THE JAPANESE ECONOMY

D0023768

WORLD ECONOMIES

A series of concise modern economic histories of the world's most important national economies. Each book explains how a country's economy
works, why it has the shape it has, and what distinct challenges it faces.
Alongside discussion of familiar indicators of economic growth, the coverage extends to well-being, inequality and corruption, to provide a fresh and
more rounded understanding of the wealth of nations.

PUBLISHED

Matthew Gray
THE ECONOMY OF THE GULF STATES

Matthew McCartney
THE INDIAN ECONOMY

Vera Zamagni
THE ITALIAN ECONOMY

Hiroaki Richard Watanabe
THE JAPANESE ECONOMY

The Japanese Economy

Hiroaki Richard Watanabe

agenda
publishing

© Hiroaki Richard Watanabe 2020

This book is copyright under the Berne Convention.
No reproduction without permission.
All rights reserved.

First edition published in 2020 by Agenda Publishing

Agenda Publishing Limited
The Core
Bath Lane
Newcastle Helix
Newcastle upon Tyne
NE4 5TF

www.agendapub.com

ISBN 978-1-78821-050-8 (hardcover)
ISBN 978-1-78821-051-5 (paperback)

British Library Cataloguing-in-Publication Data
A catalogue record for this book is available from the British Library

Typeset by Patty Rennie

Printed and bound in the UK by
CPI Group (UK) Ltd, Croydon, CR0 4YY

Contents

Preface

After defeat in the Second World War, Japan achieved an economic miracle in the 1960s. Japan also maintained relatively high economic growth in the 1970s despite two oil crises while other industrialized countries such as the United States and major European countries suffered from economic stagnation. Japan even began to threaten the dominant position of the US in the world economy during the 1980s and the Japanese economy was almost unstoppable during the bubble economy in the late 1980s. However, the Japanese economy suddenly decelerated after the collapse of the bubble economy in the early 1990s, when Japan's average stock price (Nikkei 225 Stock Price Index) dropped sharply from its highest point of around ¥40,000 to a low point of less than ¥20,000 in only a few years. Since then, Japan's economic growth has remained low and stagnant most of the time. In 2010, Japan was surpassed by China in terms of GDP size, and today the Chinese economy is more than twice the size of Japan's. The Japanese economy has experienced dramatic change, and the key turning point was the collapse of the bubble economy.

Although the change was dramatic and significant, the Japanese economy has also continued to maintain some of its core characteristics. Some of these originated a long time ago, such as its economic nationalism, which originated with the opening-up of an isolated Japan by western powers in the late Edo period. The government promoted industrialization since the Meiji Restoration in 1868 to survive the era of imperialism, with the privatization of some economic industries following later. However, the military government began to intervene in the economy extensively in the 1930s and it is during this period up to the end of the Second World War that Japan's quintessential economic characteristics, such as government–business collaboration led by economic bureaucrats, was institutionalized. With some significant transformation, a close government–business or state–market relationship still characterizes the Japanese economy. In this sense, an analysis from a political perspective is essential for examining and understanding the Japanese economy.

This book will examine the main characteristics of the Japanese economy and analyze why they exist in their current form. Chapter 1 will review the key political and economic events in Japan in chronological order. The chapter will first introduce readers to the Japanese economy before the Second World War from the end of Japan's isolation in the mid-nineteenth century up to the end of the Second World War in order to provide the necessary context for examining the main postwar developments in the Japanese economy. Close attention will be paid to the development of Japanese capitalism since the Meiji Restoration in 1868 in pursuit of imperialism and the extensive intervention in the economy by the military government in the 1930s and 1940s. The chapter will then examine the economic policy of the US occupation force, the economic miracle of the 1960s under the political dominance of the Liberal Democratic Party (LDP), the impact of the oil crises in the 1970s and the US–Japan trade disputes and the bubble economy in the 1980s. The main issue examined in this chapter is how and why Japan achieved an economic miracle in the 1960s and an analysis of the state–market relations in the management of the economy.

Chapter 2 will review the Japanese economy since the collapse of the bubble economy in the early 1990s. The chapter will examine Japan's economic stagnation in the 1990s and its own financial crisis after the Asian financial crisis of the late 1990s, the structural reform that was initiated by the non-LDP coalition government in 1994 and succeeded by the LDP's Hashimoto administration in the late 1990s, the economic deregulation implemented by the Koizumi administration in the early 2000s, the economic policy implemented by the government of the Democratic Party of Japan (DPJ) between 2009 and 2012, and "Abenomics" and its revisions by the LDP's Abe administration since December 2012. The chapter will conduct an extensive analysis of Abenomics, among other things, and assess how and why it went well and badly.

Chapter 3 measures the key elements of the Japanese economy to provide readers with a macroeconomic picture of Japan. The chapter first measures Japan's GDP, GDP growth and GDP per capita in time series and from an international comparative perspective. The chapter then measures Japan's inflation rate and labour productivity. In the second section, the chapter examines the international dimension of the Japanese economy such as exports, imports, trade balance and outward and inward FDI. In the third section, the chapter examines the government sector and measures government expenditures on social welfare, local government subsidies, public works, etc., government revenues and its components such as income tax, corporate tax, consumption tax and government bonds, and government deficits and debts, among other things. In the final section, the chapter investigates the elements of the Japanese welfare state, including pensions, healthcare, elderly (long-term) care and unemployment insurance. It will also measure socio-economic phenomena related to the welfare state such as inequality, poverty and aging population.

Chapter 4 examines the structure of the Japanese economy in terms of the state–market relationship, the complementarity among economic institutions such as *keiretsu*, convergence and diversity among capitalisms under neoliberal globalization, the dual economy, and the impact of regional economic integration on the structure of the economy. The chapter examines, among other things, the core characteristics of the Japanese "developmental state", the transformation and continuity of Japanese capitalism, the inefficiency in some economic sectors and the impact of the rise of China on Japan's international political economy.

Chapter 5 examines the Japanese economy in terms of human resources and the labour market. The chapter first deals with the changes and continuities of Japan's quintessential human resource management such as lifetime employment and seniority pay and promotion as well as cooperative industrial relations. The chapter identifies gender discrimination in the labour market and analyzes why it exists. The chapter also investigates the causes of the dual labour market in Japan and how they are changing by examining the diversification of the labour market. The chapter goes on to analyze the negative impacts of labour market deregulation since the late 1990s on working conditions and fertility rates in Japan. In this respect, union response to poor working conditions is discussed. The chapter finally examines the population decline and labour migration (both domestic and international) as a solution to revitalize the local economies.

Chapter 6 identifies Japan's "Galapagos" syndrome: economic and business practices that are a feature of the Japanese economy which do not meet global standards. The chapter examines the lack of digitalization and the inefficiency in some economic sectors that have contributed to the maintenance of Galapagos Japan. Chapter 7, the concluding chapter, assesses the prospects and challenges for the Japanese economy in future years by re-examining some of the issues identified in previous chapters such as the low fertility rate and the impact of the rise of China as well as assessing the sustainability of the Japanese welfare state.

This book, throughout, aims to identify and examine the myths and realities of the Japanese economy. The final chapter on Galapagos Japan is particularly relevant in this respect. In addition to my research experience of Japanese and comparative political economy and international relations in East Asia and the Asia Pacific, my teaching experience at the University of Sheffield, my time as an Erasmus scholar at three European universities (University of Duisburg, Autonomous University of Barcelona and Ca Foscari, University of Venice), and at the University of San Francisco as the Kiriyama Professor has helped me sharpen my understanding of the Japanese economy and was useful for writing this book. Invited talks at several institutions, including universities, Japan-related organizations, labour unions and consulting firms has also provided me with opportunities to teach the Japanese economy to both a general audience and professionals and were rewarding experiences.

Throughout this book, Japanese names are mentioned with the last name first and the first name second in accordance with the Japanese practice.

I would like to thank Agenda Publishing, especially Andrew Lockett, for providing me with the opportunity to write a book on the Japanese economy. This book had not been born without his assistance and encouragement. I would also like to thank Steven Gerrard for his comments on an earlier draft, which much improved its arguments and readability. The comments of anonymous reviewers were also extremely constructive and helpful.

Finally, I would like to show my love and gratitude to three most important women in my life: my mother, my daughter and my wife. Although my mother lives in Tokyo and I cannot see her often, we communicate frequently, and she is always willing to help me. My daughter, Erika Larissa Rafaela, is the most lovable and funniest woman I have ever met and gives me the biggest joy of my life. My wife, Natasha, has always been patient with me and provided moral support. I dedicate this book to these three women.

HIROAKI RICHARD WATANABE
London

Tables and Figures

Map of Japan

Source: Rainer Lesniewski / Alamy Stock Vector.

1

Introducing the Japanese economy

In the modern imperial period after the Meiji Restoration in 1868, the Japanese government attempted to develop the economy by promoting the national slogan of "rich nation, strong army". It was the manifestation of economic nationalism in response to western imperialism. Japan began the process of industrialization with the government leadership in the Meiji era, but later private sectors acquired greater scope of business freedom. However, after Japan suffered from a severe economic depression in the late 1920s, the military government began to intervene in the economy in the early 1930s. Eventually, the Japanese economy was devastated during the Second World War. After Japan's defeat, the United States, which led the Allied Powers, occupied Japan and postwar Japan began its economic reconstruction. The US occupation force implemented several reforms to demilitarize and democratize Japan, including the enactment of a new democratic constitution that proclaimed that sovereign power resides with the people and that renounced war as a sovereign right of the nation. However, its focus moved to the strengthening of Japan as a counter-communism force against a background of the intensification of the Cold War. After achieving independence in 1952, Japan under the Liberal Democratic Party (LDP) attempted to remilitarize Japan by amending a new constitution in the 1950s. However, this aim did not materialize. Since then, Japan focused on economic growth and achieved its "economic miracle" in the 1960s. Despite a slowdown due to the oil crises, the Japanese economy continued to grow in the 1970s and had a frenzied period of growth in the bubble economy in the late 1980s. Since 1955, when the LDP was created, Japan maintained political stability under the political dominance of the LDP (called the "1955 system") until 1993. This political stability provided a favourable condition for economic growth in postwar Japan.

This chapter will introduce the Japanese economy by beginning with an analysis of the major developments of Japanese capitalism in the pre-war era. The chapter will examine government economic policy after the Meiji Restoration, Japan's industrialization with *zaibatsu* economic conglomerates as an important economic actor, and the war-time planned economy of the 1930s until the end of the Second World War based on the extensive intervention in the economy by the military government. The chapter will then examine the formation of the postwar economy until the collapse of the bubble economy in the early 1990s. The chapter will periodize the postwar economy between 1945 and 1990 into: 1) economic reconstruction after Japan's defeat in the Second World War (1945–late 1950s); 2) economic miracle in the 1960s; 3) lower economic growth in the 1970s as a result of the oil crises; and 4) trade conflict with the US and the bubble economy of the 1980s. The chapter will examine the impact of the US occupation policy and the "Yoshida doctrine" on the formation of the postwar economy in the first period and then the factors that contributed to Japan's economic miracle in the 1960s from the perspective of state–market relations (e.g. government intervention in the economy with the industrial policy implemented by the Ministry of International Trade and Industry (MITI) and business practices). The chapter will then discuss the economic slowdown of the 1970s despite the relatively good performance of the economy compared to western economies. The chapter will highlight that this led to western admiration of the Japanese economy, especially Japan's industrial relations, and the emergence of the nationalistic *nihonjinron* (theory of Japanese-ness), which emphasized Japanese uniqueness and superiority. Finally, the chapter will discuss

Japan's trade imbalance with the United States and the economic bubble of the late 1980s.

PRE-SECOND WORLD WAR ECONOMY

Since the mid-seventeenth century, the ruling Bakufu (military government) of the Tokugawa dynasty in Japan had closed the country from the outside world to prevent the spread of Christian influence and to monopolize trade with foreign countries (Elisonas 1991). However, in 1854, Japan was finally forced to open-up the country by Commodore Matthew Perry of the United States, who visited Japan in formidable battleships and threatened the Bakufu with possible attack should they refuse to open the country. Japan was forced to conclude the Friendship Treaty with the US and opened the country. Similar treaties with Russia, Britain and the Netherlands were concluded soon later. After signing the Friendship Treaty, the US sought to enter into a commercial treaty with Japan and the US–Japan Commercial Treaty was concluded in 1858. It was an unfair treaty from the Japanese perspective in two respects: firstly, Japan did not have autonomy to decide its own tariff rates, and secondly, Japan was required to hire foreign judges when foreigners were indicted. Japan later concluded similar commercial treaties with Russia, Britain, France and the Netherlands.[1]

The opening of trade relationships had a great impact on the Japanese economy. Japan's main export products included raw silk and tea and its main import products included woollen fabric, cotton cloth and military products (see Figure 1.1). While the growth of raw silk exports promoted the silk industry, the import of a large amount of cotton cloth negatively affected the domestic cotton textile industry (Beasley 1989: 306; Hane 1992: 69–70; Jansen 1989: 340). In addition, the difference in the ratios between gold and silver in Japan (1:5) and overseas (1:15) enabled foreign merchants to purchase gold much more cheaply in Japan and sell it more expensively outside Japan. As a result, a large amount of gold outflowed overseas from Japan (Hane 1992: 70). In response, the Bakufu reduced the

Figure 1.1 Japan's exports and imports after the end of isolation in 1865

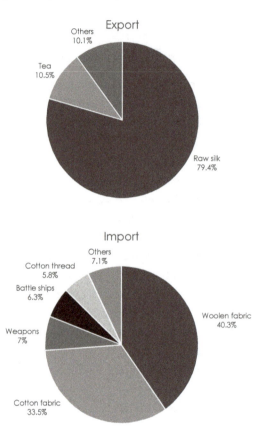

Source: Ishii (1994).

amount of gold in coins but this devaluation led to a hyperinflation. This created ill-feeling towards foreign trade among Japan's military nobility, the *samurai*, and led to the emergence of a radical philosophy and movement called *son-nō jō-i* (revere the emperor, expel foreign barbarians). However, *jō-i* (expel foreign barbarians) was replaced with *tōbaku* (defeat the Bakufu) after fanatic *samurai* warriors realized the impossibility of expelling western imperial powers and sought to blame the Bakufu instead for opening the country. Eventually, southern and western provinces of Satsuma and Chōshū formed a military coalition and conducted a *coup d'état* to oust the Bakufu from power. Although the last Shōgun Yoshinobu proposed to surrender power to the imperial court on the condition that a government centered on the Tokugawa clan would be formed in coalition with *daimyō* provincial lords, Satsuma and Chōshū announced the establishment of a new government centered on the Emperor (Hall 1971: 263–4; Hane 1992: 80–81). The new government defeated the Bakufu forces and the Tokugawa dynasty ended in 1868 with the restoration of power to the Emperor (Meiji Restoration). Edo was renamed Tokyo and replaced Kyoto as the new capital (the location of the imperial palace) of Japan in 1869.

The new government in the Meiji period (1868–1911) adopted the national slogan of the "rich nation, strong army" to survive the era of imperialism and attempted to industrialize the country. For this purpose, the feudalistic socio-economic system was abolished. The government also invited foreign technicians to introduce new technologies and develop the infrastructure. For example, the first railroads connecting large cities such as Tokyo and Yokohama and then Kyoto, Osaka and Kobe were built (Crawcour 1989b: 394). The government also introduced foreign technologies to build factories to spin and produce a large amount of silk and cotton threads and yarns so that Japan would be able to increase exports of those products (Hane 1992: 99). In the process of promoting industrialization, private business families (merchant houses in the Edo period) such as Mitsui and Iwasaki (later Mitsubishi) were provided with several privileges and were called *seishō* (government merchants).

Matsukata Masayoshi, who became Finance Minister in 1881, established the Bank of Japan as the central bank in 1882. Matsukata implemented a deflationary policy and Japan experienced economic recession with a sharp drop in the prices of goods, including rice (Crawcour 1989a: 614–15; Hall 1971: 305–06). As a result, many farmers became tenants and borrowed land from landholders, who enriched themselves by both charging high tenant fees and engaging in money lending at the same time. The emergence of many poor tenants in villages as well as poor former lower-class *samurai* created social disturbance (Hane 1992: 100). However, after the implementation of Matsukata's deflation policy, Japanese exports surpassed imports and there was a boom of establishing companies in the industrial sectors such as railroad and cotton spinning due to an increase in company stock transactions (the beginning of Japan's "industrial revolution"). With a large amount of indemnity from a victory in the first Sino-Japanese War in 1894–95, the government promoted light and heavy industries by introducing the gold standard and establishing special banks such as the Industrial Bank of Japan for long-term investment and the Yokohama Specie Bank for trade finance.

It was the textile industry, through technical innovation, that occupied the central position in the establishment of Japanese capitalism (Taira 1989: 606). In 1883, Osaka Cotton Spinning Corporation began to produce cotton thread by using imported machines and steam engines, and Japan's export of cotton thread to destinations such as China and Korea surpassed imports by 1897 (Crawcour 1989b: 423–25; Hane 1992: 140–43). After the Russo-Japanese War in 1904–05, large corporations in a monopolistic position exported cotton thread to the Manchurian market too. However, it was the silk industry that played the largest role in Japan's acquisition of foreign currencies. Silk thread was the largest of Japan's export goods and was exported to Europe and North America. Many small factories in agricultural areas produced silk thread and later silk textiles. Japan even surpassed China as the largest exporter of silk thread in 1909.

The government privatized public corporations except military and railroad companies and the *seishō* acquired several businesses including mining. These wealthy business families such as Mitsui and Mitsubishi grew further to become the *zaibatsu* (business conglomerates) engaged in several businesses across finance, trade, transport, mining and others. For example, Mitsui operated Miike Mine in Kyushu, the largest coal mine in Japan, and Mitsubishi built a large ship building factory in Nagasaki (Hane 1992: 100–101). However, to facilitate military expansion, the government began to operate Yawata Steel Factory in 1901 and nationalized the production of steel, considered necessary for the development of heavy industry (Hane 1992: 142). With an increasing demand for machinery from heavy industry as well as cotton necessary for the spinning industry, Japan's imports exceeded exports by a large margin once again and its trade deficit increased to a critical level.

After the Russo-Japanese War, the overseas markets in Manchuria, where Japan acquired greater influence, and Korea, which Japan colonized in 1910, increased their importance for the Japanese economy. In the domestic market, many farmers became involved in the production of commercial agricultural products with a growth of Japanese capitalism. While landowners became "parasitic" (called "absentee landlords") in the sense that they relied on tenant fees for their incomes without cultivating the land themselves and invested in business and company stocks, many farmers became poor tenants. In addition, wage labourers emerged with the growth of light and heavy industries. Factory workers, who were organized and mobilized by then illegal labour unions, demanded the improvement of working conditions by conducting strikes. This led to the emergence of socialism in Japan in the late nineteenth century. However, socialist political parties were severely supressed and dissolved by the government (Hane 1992: 144–8).

The Japanese economy at the end of the Meiji period and the beginning of the ensuing Taisho period (1911–25) was in a critical situation due to economic stagnation and fiscal deficits. However, with the beginning of the First World War, Japan was able to greatly increase export of cotton textile products to Asian markets, from where European imperial powers withdrew to engage in the war in Europe (Crawcour 1989b: 436–7). Japan's export of silk thread to the US market also increased significantly. The worldwide shortage of ships and vessels allowed the ship building industry in Japan to prosper with several entrepreneurs making huge profits. With the development of steel, chemical, electricity and machinery industries, the ratio of heavy chemical industries among the secondary sector exceeded 30 per cent. Also, the number of wage labourers engaged in the secondary sector exceeded one million as a result of the growth in the heavy chemical industry.

At the beginning of the Showa era (1926–89), Japan experienced a financial crisis. In 1927, the disclosure of unhealthy financial situations of several banks resulted in panic with many depositors trying to withdraw their savings. The crisis was overcome only after the government issued a moratorium and provided rescue finance to those banks (Hane 1992: 235–6; Nakamura 1989: 456–8). However, Japan was later to experience a serious economic depression due to the fiscal restraint policy of the new administration led by Prime Minister Hamaguchi of the Minseitō Party and the Global Depression that began in the US in 1929. The Hamaguchi administration lifted the embargo on gold exports and implemented a deflationary policy to enhance the competitiveness of the Japanese economy (Nakamura 1989: 462–5). As a result, many companies went bankrupt and the number of unemployed workers increased to a significant extent. The poverty of villages also increased due to a sharp drop of agricultural products. The number of labour and peasant disputes increased as a result. Amidst this crisis, *zaibatsu*, which monopolized the economy through the control of several industries, including finance, retail and heavy chemical industries, deepened their connection with political parties. This gave rise to political corruption involving the *zaibatsu* and the parties and increased the criticism by right-wing fanatics, who included many young Japanese from poverty-stricken villages (Waswo 1989: 556). Many of them were to join the military later, as Japan saw a rise of military and right-wing fanaticism in the 1930s.

After Prime Minister Hamaguchi was physically attacked by a young right-wing fanatic in the same year (1930) of the signing of the London Naval Treaty and later died, Prime Minister Inukai of the Seiyūkai Party formed a cabinet in 1931 with Takahashi Korekiyo as Finance Minister.[2] Takahashi reversed the Hamaguchi administrations' fiscal restraint and deflationary policy and adopted a policy of fiscal expansion (so-called "Takahashi finance"). He reintroduced the embargo on gold exports and Japan's exports increased with depreciated yen. His lax fiscal policy by issuing deficit bonds stimulated the economy, and Japan escaped from economic depression before western imperial powers did (Gao 2001: 50; Nakamura 1989: 468). The government policy to expand the military and protect strategic industries contributed to the rapid growth of heavy chemical industry in the 1930s (see Figure 1.2). For example, the government merged steel companies to create a national champion called *Nihon Seitetsu Gaisha* (Japan Steel Corporation). As a result, the production of steel increased. In addition, many waged workers moved into the heavy chemical industry on an unprecedented scale (Taira 1989: 611). The government also increased economic control by enacting the Important Industry Control Law in 1931 that mandated cartels (Gao 2001: 51).

Figure 1.2 Japan's manufacturing composition, 1919–38

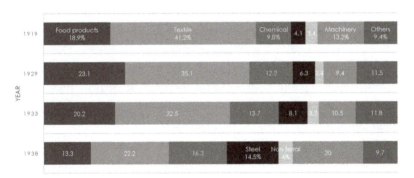

Source: Shinohara (2014).

In 1931, the Kwantung Army stationed in Manchuria invaded the region against government wishes and established a puppet state of Manchukuo (the "Manchurian Incident"). Manchukuo was administered by the military officers of the Kwantung Army and by the reformist bureaucrats who originally denounced the *zaibatsu* capitalism. They engaged in the planned management of Manchukuo's economy in collaboration with "new" *zaibatsu* such as Nissan, not with traditional *zaibatsu* such as Mitsui and Mitsubishi (Nakamura 1989: 471–80). Nissan, one of the new *zaibatsu* that emerged in the 1930s, advanced to Manchuria and monopolized the heavy chemical industry in the region. The Manchurian incident encouraged right-wing officers and fanatics in Japan to take direct action, and a group of young navy officers shot and killed Prime Minister Inukai in May 15, 1932 ("5.15 Incident"). Critical of political parties and the *zaibatsu* for their corruption and the dire poverty in rural villages, they were determined to establish a military dictatorship, and continued terrorist activities after the May 15 incident. On February 26, 1936, young army officers attacked the prime minister's office and police headquarters and killed several senior politicians and army generals, including Finance Minister Takahashi Korekiyo ("2.26 Incident").

With the demise of party government after the May 15 Incident, the government came under the strong influence of the military, which began to intervene in the economy to pursue its military expansionist aims, for example, by passing special laws to promote the development of the heavy chemical industry and the oil and machine tools industries (Nakamura 1989: 473). Despite the greater control of the economy by the military government that began to undermine business autonomy from politics, the *zaibatsu* increased cooperation with the military government to expand their business in the heavy chemical industry.

With the beginning of the second Sino-Japanese War in 1937, the Cabinet of Prime Minister Konoe began to implement direct government control of the economy by enacting special laws related to the government budget and international trade. The Cabinet Planning Board (*Kikakuin*) was established in 1937 for the purpose of regulating the supply and demand of major commodities necessary for war-time controlled economic activities and drawing up an economic mobilization plan (Nakamura 1989: 481). In 1938, the Konoe Cabinet enacted the National Mobilization Law and the government acquired the authority to intervene in the national economy without Diet (Parliament) approval. The government prioritized the production of military goods by allocating to it a large amount of the government budget and by using most of the imported materials for that purpose. In this way, the *zaibatsu* increased production of military goods in cooperation with the military government. Labour unions were also reorganized into the Industrial Patriotic Associations (*Sangyō Hōkokukai*) and performance-based pay was rejected. Instead, the so-called "livelihood" wage, which later became seniority-based pay, was introduced (Gao 2001: 54–5).

Japan attacked Pearl Harbor in Hawaii in December 1941 and the Pacific War between the US and Japan began. The Cabinet of Prime Minister Tōjō claimed that the main purpose of Japan's engagement in the Second World War was to free Asia from western imperial powers and the establishment of the Great East Asia Co-prosperity Sphere was announced. However, this announcement was no more than rhetoric and Japan's real aim was to acquire a greater amount of the raw materials necessary for producing military goods in the expanded territories. After defeat in the Battle of Midway in June 1942, Japan began to lose the war with the US and recede from its empire. The Tōjō Cabinet fell after the fall of Saipan in July 1944 and the US began air bombing on mainland Japan. However, even after the announcement of the Potsdam Declaration by the Allied powers of the US, Britain and China that threatened the total annihilation of Japan without its unconditional surrender and the later atomic bombings of Hiroshima and Nagasaki in August 1945, fanatical elements of the Japanese military were still not ready to surrender. It was only after the Soviet Union's participation in the war against Japan and its advancement into Manchuria and Korea that Emperor Hirohito announced the acceptance of the Potsdam Declaration and unconditional surrender. Japan's reckless continuation of a hopeless war utterly destroyed its economy.

ECONOMIC RECONSTRUCTION AFTER THE SECOND WORLD WAR

After Japan's surrender in the Second World War, the US-led Allied Powers occupied Japan, with Douglas MacArthur as the Supreme Commander for the Allied Powers (SCAP). The US did not implement direct military control of Japan but relied on Japanese bureaucracy to implement several reforms to demilitarize and democratize Japan more efficiently (Fukui 1989: 180–81). The Japanese military was disbanded, and war criminals were arrested and indicted, with some executed. In addition, many politicians and *zaibatsu* leaders who were thought to have cooperated with the military were purged from their official positions.

SCAP ordered to freeze the assets of former *zaibatsu* such as Mitsui, Mitsubishi and Sumitomo and acquired their company stocks. In 1947, SCAP enacted the Anti-Trust Law, which banned shareholding companies and monopoly through trust and cartel. In addition, SCAP enacted legislation to divide large monopolistic companies. However, with the advent of the Cold War, this law was not implemented sufficiently. Later, the former *zaibatsu* banks formed business groups called "*keiretsu*" (literally meaning "lineage") through mutual shareholding and financing (Kōsai 1989: 497). In addition, the Anti-Trust Law was relaxed with several amendments once Japan regained independence in 1952 (Fukui 1989: 159). Business federations were also established, such as the Committee for Economic Development (Keizai Dōyūkai) and the Japan Federation of Economic Organizations (Keidanren) in 1946 and the Japan Federation of Employer Associations (Nikkeiren), which was mostly in charge of industrial relations, in 1948 (Watanabe 2014).

As for labour policy, the Labour Union Law enacted in 1945 ensured workers' rights to unite and form unions, engage in collective bargaining and strike. As a result, three major national union confederations were formed in 1946: the left-wing National Congress of Industrial Unions (Sanbetsu), the right-wing Japan National Federation of Labour (Sōdōmei), and the centrist Japan Labour Union Congress (Nichirō Kaigi). Soon after the outbreak of the Korean War in 1950, a new national labour union confederation called the General Council of Japanese Trade Unions (Sōhyō) was formed and occupied the dominant position in the Japanese labour movement until the mid-1970s, when the International Metal Federation–Japan Council (IMF-JC) of the Sōdōmei acquired a leadership role in Japan's labour movement (Kume 1998: 128–42; 2005: 173–84). The Labour Standards Law, which is considered the constitution on labour relations, was enacted in 1947. And in the same year, the Ministry of Labour was established.

In agriculture, democratic reforms aimed at increasing the number of small-scale independent farmers were implemented. Before the end of the war, a relatively small number of landlords, who did not engage in farming themselves, held most of the land and leased it to tenants ("absentee-landlordism"). As absent-landlordism was considered a main cause for the spread of poverty and a rise of fanatic nationalism in rural villages, SCAP ordered the Japanese government to purchase all land held by landlords and to distribute this to peasants at affordable prices to enable a large number of tenants to become independent farmers. With this process, landlords lost their economic and social privileges.

After Japan's surrender, many Japanese soldiers who were fighting overseas and Japanese residents in former Japanese colonies such as Taiwan, Korea and Manchukuo returned to Japan. With the collapse of military-related industries, there were few employment opportunities for them and along with most Japanese who escaped and survived the US bombing, they suffered from dire poverty and hunger despite the end of hostilities. In addition, a severe lack of goods caused hyperinflation and increased the level of distress among Japanese people.

In 1947, the Japanese government allocated government funds raised through the issue of deficit bonds exclusively to the production of steel, which was considered the most important resource for industrial development. This was called the "priority production method" ("*keisha seisan hōshiki*") (Fukui 1989: 180; Kōsai 1989: 500–01; Okazaki 1999: 235–43). Although this policy along with the policy to restrain wage hikes contributed to an increase in industrial production, it further escalated inflation and led to an increase in the number of labour disputes and strikes.

The first phase of the US occupation policy was based on the demilitarization and democratization of Japan so that Japan would never again become a threat to international peace. To this end, the US implemented policies to restrain the economic reconstruction of Japan. However, due to the intensification of the Cold War, the US reversed its economic policy towards Japan and began to implement policies that strengthened the Japanese economy so that Japan would be able to become a reliable capitalist ally. In Northeast Asia, the Cold War situation intensified with the division of the Korean peninsula between capitalist South Korea and communist North Korea in 1948 and the emergence of communist China on the mainland in 1949. In this political situation, the US also reversed its demilitarization and democratization policy towards Japan (called the "reverse course"), as seen in a communist purge ("red purge") and the restoration of formerly purged (right-wing) politicians and *zaibatsu* leaders to their previous official positions just before the beginning of the Korean War in 1950 (Fukui 1989: 158).

In December 1948, the US ordered the Japanese government to implement nine economic policies to stabilize the economy, including a balanced budget, wage stabilization and price control. Later, the US instructed the government to implement a balanced budget without any deficit and sent to Japan Joseph Dodge, the former chairman of the Detroit Bank (the so-called "Dodge Line") (Fukui 1989: 177; Kōsai 1989: 502). The US also sent the economist Carl Shoup to radically revise Japan's tax system. With these economic measures, the US aimed to restrain the hyperinflation (125 per cent in 1947) and build a basis for economic reconstruction (Kōsai 1989: 502). Although the hyperinflation began to abate and the official exchange rate of $1.00 = ¥360 was set, Japan suffered a serious economic depression (stabilization crisis). As a result, many small- and middle-sized companies went bankrupt and the number of the unemployed increased in both private and public sectors. As a measure to cope with an increasing number of labour disputes and strikes, the Japanese government issued Cabinet Order 201 based on the order by SCAP, which deprived national civil servants of the right to strike. In this political and economic climate, labour unions were divided into left-wing and right-wing factions and their power was weakened.

The Korean War, which had begun in 1950, revived the Japanese economy. Japan functioned as a US military base and an increase in the US demand for Japanese military goods to engage in the war contributed to the recovery of the economy. In addition, with a national policy of the allocation of government funds to basic industries such as steel, shipbuilding and electricity, the economy began to grow rapidly. In 1952, Japan joined the International Monetary Fund (IMF) and the World Bank.

Against the geopolitical background of the intensification of the Cold War and the beginning of the Korean War, the United States expedited the independence of Japan as a reliable US ally. With the signing of the San Francisco Peace Treaty with the US and 47 other countries in 1951, Japan achieved independence in the following year and the US occupation of Japan ended. At the same time of the signing of the San Francisco Peace Treaty, the United States and Japan concluded the US–Japan Security Treaty, which enabled the US to maintain its military bases in Japan.

After the end of the US occupation of Japan in 1952, conservative right-wing politicians who returned to politics demanded Japan's remilitarization and constitutional changes. Article 9 of the new Constitution enacted in 1947 stipulated the denunciation of war and no military capability. Prime Minister Yoshida Shigeru, who had served as prime minister during the US occupation and after the independence of Japan, established the Self-Defence Force in 1954. However, Yoshida resisted demands for remilitarization from the US and Japanese conservative right-wing politicians. Instead, he focused on economic reconstruction by relying on the US for Japan's security based on the US–Japan Security Treaty. This policy, known as the "Yoshida Doctrine", constrained the attempts of remilitarization by some LDP prime ministers during and after the Cold War.

After the resignation of Prime Minister Yoshida in December 1954, the Liberal Democratic Party (LDP) was formed in 1955 as a result of the merger between the Liberal Party and the Democratic Party. The first LDP Prime Minister Hatoyama Ichirō attempted to remilitarize Japan by amending Article 9 of the Constitution. At the same time, he improved Japan's relation with the Soviet Union by signing in 1956 the Japan–Soviet Joint Declaration to end the war between the two countries. The LDP maintained a little less than two-thirds majority of the Diet (Parliament) seats while the Socialist Party, which was also formed in 1955, maintained a little more than one-third of the Diet seats, which was necessary for preventing the LDP from proposing a national referendum for a constitutional amendment.[3] This political situation based on LDP dominance became known as the "1955 system" and lasted until the formation of a non-LDP coalition government in 1993 (Kitaoka 1995).

After the resignation of Prime Minister Hatoyama and his successor Prime Minister Ishibashi, Prime Minister Kishi Nobusuke, who also wanted to achieve Japan's remilitarization through a constitutional amendment, attempted to strengthen Japan's self-defence by amending the US–Japan Security Treaty. The original Treaty did not stipulate the US obligation to defend Japan despite the US right to station its military force in Japan, but the amended Treaty fixed this problem by stipulating such US obligation. Despite the strong opposition from the progressive forces such as the opposition Socialist Party, the Communist Party and university students, the Kishi administration resisted such opposition and pushed through the measure in the Diet. Amidst the chaotic political climate, the new US–Japan Security Treaty became effective in 1960. However, Prime Minister Kishi was forced to resign soon after.

ECONOMIC MIRACLE IN THE 1960S UNDER THE GOVERNMENT OF THE LIBERAL DEMOCRATIC PARTY

Prime Minister Ikeda Hayato, who succeeded Kishi in 1960, learnt from the Kishi administration's mistakes and avoided contentious political issues such as remilitarization and constitutional amendment. Instead, Ikeda focused on the economy and reverted to the Yoshida Doctrine: pursuing economic growth by relying on the US for Japan's security.

Prime Minister Ikeda announced the "Income Doubling Plan" and implemented economic policies aimed at high economic growth. Despite economic pundits doubting the achievement of income doubling, the national income more than doubled. Japan achieved an "economic miracle" of more than 10 per cent of annual GDP growth until the Japanese economy was hit by the oil crises in the 1970s. It was both the growth of the domestic market and an increase in exports that enabled the Japanese economy to grow rapidly in the 1960s. With the growth in the manufacturing sector due to technological improvement and greater competitiveness, workers' wages grew, and their purchasing power also grew.[4] This created a virtuous circle of more production, more spending and more investment. Manufacturing production also increased due to the growth in exports. With a fixed exchange rate of $1.00 to ¥360, under which Japanese yen was undervalued, and with the availability of cheap imported raw materials, Japanese manufacturing companies were able to increase their exports and Japan as a result achieved a huge trade surplus. While heavy chemical industry products such as steel, automobiles and ships occupied more than two-thirds of exports, oil and raw materials to produce heavy chemical products occupied a majority of imports.

Among the most important actors in the government sector that contributed to the economic miracle was the Ministry of International Trade and Industry (MITI). MITI implemented industrial policy to promote the growth of strategic sectors such as steel and petrochemicals by providing subsidies and allocating scarce foreign currencies to those sectors (Johnson 1982). Although the "administrative guidance", through which MITI implemented the industrial policy, did not have the power of legal enforcement, the business sector often had to compromise and follow the guidance as it had "de facto" legal status. There were a small number of notable exceptions, however, such as the resistance by the automobile sector to the government plan to merge car companies to create a national champion with greater international competitiveness (Kume 2000: 78–9). Also, in addition to MITI's industrial policy, we cannot ignore the importance of the wider international political economy during the Cold War. To keep Japan as a capitalist ally and maintain its military bases there, the US kept its domestic market wide open to Japan despite Japan's closed market and absorbed a large amount of Japanese exports (Pempel 1999a: 146–7, 179).

One of the distinctive features of Japan's economy – the close cooperation and coordination in the management of the economy between government and business sectors – originated in the war-time economy (Nakamura 1989: 481; Noguchi 1998). As mentioned above, the military government needed to increase the production of military goods and began to intervene in the economy to a significant extent by demanding the former *zaibatsu* to follow the government economic plan. After the end of the war, the US occupation force implemented several reform policies. While conservative right-wing politicians and *zaibatsu* leaders who were considered to have cooperated with the military regime were purged, bureaucrats were not. This is because the US relied on Japanese bureaucracy for implementing those reform policies (Fukui 1989: 180–81). As a result, bureaucrats did not lose but maintained the power to intervene in the economy, which they had acquired during the war-time economy. This legacy of government intervention continued after the end of the war, and MITI bureaucrats performed an important role in the achievement of high economic growth in the 1960s.

OIL CRISES AND SLOWER ECONOMIC GROWTH IN THE 1970S

The high economic growth in the 1960s suddenly ended due to the oil crises in the 1970s. While the Japanese economy continued growing most of the time in the 1970s, the growth rate became far lower than in the previous decade. Japan heavily relied on imports of oil as an energy source and the dramatic rise in oil prices had a negative impact on the growth of the economy. In addition, Japan was forced to move to a floating exchange rate in 1973 and the yen appreciated as a result. The higher-valued yen reduced the competitiveness of Japanese low-priced exports, highlighting the need to increase production and exports of higher value-added products. The late 1970s was also the time when newly industrializing economies (NIEs) such as South Korea and Taiwan emerged and increasingly became competitors of Japanese exports.

To cope with the 400 per cent hike in oil prices due to the Arab–Israeli War and the first oil crisis in 1973 and Japan's first negative GDP growth in 1974, Prime Minister Tanaka Kakuei relied on public works to stimulate the economy even by issuing deficit bonds for the first time since the Second World War. Tanaka announced the launch of the "Japanese Archipelago Reconstruction Plan" and implemented many infrastructure projects, and even those that did not have economic rationality in terms of cost performance were implemented as "political" projects. LDP's *zoku* (policy tribe) politicians, who had expertise in a specific policy area and maintained close links with the interest groups as their political supporters, promoted political construction projects by consulting with the relevant ministries so that they could maintain their supporters and get votes at the time of elections (Inoguchi & Iwai 1987). In fact, Tanaka himself was a well-known construction *zoku* politician and achieved promotion during his political career by engaging in construction projects. Public works also functioned as a kind of "welfare" or employment policy by providing jobs to construction workers irrespective of whether public works projects had an economic rational or not (Kitaoka 1995: 140–56). It was not the same as the western-style traditional welfare but it suited the Japanese "developmental state", where economic growth, not social welfare, was the number one priority of the government.[5] However, the promotion of public works created many corruptions and reduced people's trust in politics and the government. It also exacerbated the government's fiscal deficits.

The second oil crisis occurred in 1979 as a result of the Iranian Revolution. As in the case of the first oil crisis in 1973, the second oil crisis, with a 300 per cent increase in oil prices, had a damaging impact on the Japanese economy. However, in contrast to the Tanaka administration that increased government spending on public works, the administration of Prime Minister Ōhira Masayoshi at the time of the second oil crisis attempted to reduce government debts that had been accumulated since the issue of the deficit bonds by the Tanaka administration. In order to achieve the balanced budget, Ōhira sought to introduce a consumption tax and announced the introduction of "Japanese-style welfare", which emphasized the role of families and individuals rather than the state in social welfare.[6] However, the "construction" state remained and continued

19

to play an important role in promoting a Japanese-style welfare state by providing jobs to those in the construction industry.

During the 1970s the Japanese economy nevertheless still performed better than the economies of major western countries such as the United State and became the second largest economy in the world by surpassing the GDP of then West Germany. It was at this time that the ideas of so-called "*nihonjinron*" (theory of Japanese-ness), which positively emphasized Japan's cultural uniqueness and economic superiority in contrast to previous ideas that emphasized its backwardness, appeared and became popular inside and outside Japan (Okumura 1994: 48–9). In Japan, the literature was highly subjective and nationalistic and in western countries it was naïve and ignorant. One of the best-known examples was Ezra Vogel's *Japan as No.1* (Vogel 1979). As can be guessed from the title of the book, Vogel pointed to uniquely Japanese characteristics that he believed contributed to Japan's economic prosperity such as high level of basic education (Ishizawa 1997: 48–67; Kageyama 1994: 109–31; Aoki 1990: 129–33). However, with hindsight, some of the Japanese characteristics that Vogel praised are now considered to have contributed to Japan's economic stagnation and social problems. Characteristics assessed by Vogel to be extremely positive such as collectivism (such as a lack of egoism and pursuit of collective benefits), bureaucracy (such as the close relationship of bureaucrats with private business and politicians) and employment practices (such as lifetime employment) were viewed rather differently after the collapse of the bubble economy: collectivism has often been considered to be detrimental to business innovation, the close relationship between bureaucrats and private business has caused numerous corruptions, and lifetime employment has contributed to overwork, gender discrimination in the labour market and insufficient transfer of human resources from declining to new economic sectors. Some of his positive statements on Japanese characteristics are overly exaggerated but contributed to an increase in confidence, or even overconfidence, among Japanese about themselves.

THE US–JAPAN TRADE CONFLICT
AND THE "BUBBLE ECONOMY" IN THE 1980S

Due to the issuing of deficit bonds to cope with the oil crises, the government debts accumulated during the 1970s. Faced with this situation, Prime Minister Nakasone Yasuhiro (1982–87) sought to reduce fiscal deficits by implementing fiscal and administrative reform. In order to achieve a balanced budget, the government needed to cut fiscal spending on public works and social welfare. Resistance to such reforms by relevant interest groups, LDP *zoku* politicians and ministries was easily anticipated. To avoid their resistance, Nakasone set up a Cabinet advisory council called the second *Rinchō* (provisional administrative reform council) that would enable him to introduce more top-down policymaking in contrast to the traditional bottom-up policymaking led by bureaucrats and *zoku* politicians. With this new Cabinet council, the Nakasone administration managed to some extent to reduce the government debts that had been accumulated since the 1970s by implementing an austerity fiscal policy such as the budget reduction for public works and social welfare. The Nakasone administration also privatized three public corporations: the national railways, the telephone and telegraphic monopoly and the tobacco monopoly. The railways, for example, had inefficient operation and accumulated debts and their privatization helped the government to reduce government debt levels. The Nakasone administration also attempted tax reform: the introduction of a consumption tax. However, it gave up on this plan due to strong opposition from inside the LDP and its political support groups such as small retailers.

The Japanese economy continued to perform well in the 1980s and the trade friction between the US and Japan became a serious political issue due to the US's huge trade deficit with Japan. From the 1950s to the 1970s, the US government had demanded Japan's "voluntary export restraint" ("VER") of such goods as textile products (1950s), steel (1960s) and televisions and automobile (1970s) to reduce the US trade deficit with Japan. However, the US government also demanded Japan's "voluntary import expansion" (VIE) in the 1980s to cope with the increased trade deficits by increasing US exports to Japan (Nakagawa 2006: 315). The US complained, for example, that American semi-conductor products could not get access to the Japanese market because of its closed nature and that Japanese semi-conductor companies had engaged in anti-competitive measures such as over-investment in production capacity and "dumping" their products on the US market by utilizing the huge profits gained from the high prices in the domestic Japanese market (Nakagawa 2006: 315–16). The US also increased calls for the liberalization of Japan's import of US agricultural products such as rice and beef. In this political context, the Plaza Accord was reached in 1985. Japanese yen (and the German Deutche mark) appreciated against the US dollar so that Japanese exports to the US market would decrease. Later, between 1989 and 1990, the US–Japan Structural Impediments Initiative was introduced. The US demanded the structural reform of the Japanese economy to eliminate unfair business practices such as self-imposed regulations and procedures, complex supply chains and business transactions based on *keiretsu* in certain economic sectors, which functioned as non-tariff barriers (NTBs) to foreign companies' entry to the Japanese market (Okumura 1994: 64–5). As a result, the Japanese government was required to revise the Large-Scale Retail Shop Law and strengthen the implementation of the Anti-Monopoly Law. The US government claimed that the Large-Scale Retail Shop Law had deterred American retailers from entering the Japanese market because of its protective measures for small Japanese retail shops. It also claimed that the lax implementation of the Anti-Monopoly Law by the Japanese government had contributed to anti-competitive measures in business sectors such as cartels and *dangō* (price rigging) (Nakagawa 2006: 318).

The appreciation of Japanese yen as a result of the Plaza Accord caused a minor recession in the Japanese economy and prompted the Bank of Japan (BOJ) to decrease interest rates in order to stimulate the economy. However, the lower interest rate policy of the BOJ led to stock and land speculations and caused the "bubble economy", which was a period of frenetic economic activity in the late 1980s created by skyrocketing increases

Figure 1.3 Nikkei stock average in the late 1980s and early 1990s

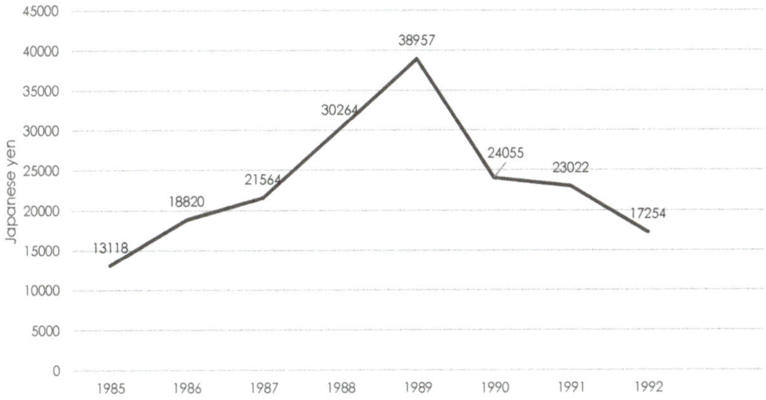

Source: Nikkei Indexes; https://indexes.nikkei.co.jp/en/nkave/archives/data.
Note: High on the last day of transaction each year.

in stock and land prices. At one time in the late 1980s, the Nikkei stock average approached the ¥40,000 benchmark (see Figure 1.3), and the land value of the Imperial Palace in the center of Tokyo became higher than the whole state of California, which is larger than Japan, for example. The Japanese economy performed well with a large amount of investment during the bubble economy in the late 1980s. However, with the dramatic drop of the Nikkei stock average to as low as less than ¥20,000 in the early 1990s after a series of interest rate hikes by the BOJ to tighten the bubble economy, it collapsed. The growth of the Japanese economy then began to decelerate and has remained stagnant ever since.

2

The transformation of the Japanese economy since the early 1990s

Japan has experienced a stagnant economy since the collapse of the bubble economy in the early 1990s. Several structural reforms have been implemented to stimulate the economy by the LDP-led coalition governments, most notably by the Hashimoto administration in the 1990s, the Koizumi administration in the 2000s and at the time of writing, the second Abe administration. As a result, the Japanese economy has experienced some significant transformations. However, it has also maintained some old characteristics.

This chapter will first examine the economic stagnation in the 1990s after the collapse of the bubble economy with reference to non-performing loans and the Asian financial crisis of 1997-98. It will discuss the economic reforms that were initiated by the non-LDP coalition government between 1993-94 and were succeeded by the LDP's Hashimoto administration in the late 1990s. The chapter will then examine the economic reforms implemented by the Koizumi administration in the first half of the 2000s, followed by an analysis of the impact of the global financial crisis in 2008 and the economic policy of the government of the Democratic Party of Japan (DPJ) between 2009 and 2012. Finally, the chapter will discuss the "Abenomics" of the current Abe administration as its economic growth strategy.

ECONOMIC STAGNATION AFTER THE COLLAPSE OF THE
BUBBLE ECONOMY AND REGULATORY REFORMS IN THE 1990S

Stock prices, which Japanese people believed would continue rising forever, suddenly dropped sharply in 1990. Land prices also started to drop at a dramatic rate. As a result of sharp declines of stock and land prices, investment came to a standstill and so began the decades of economic stagnation and low economic growth. Many Japanese companies that had borrowed excessively from banks without due diligence during the years of the bubble economy went bankrupt, as they could not repay loans with stocks or land as collaterals that were now devalued with the collapse of the bubble economy. As a result, Japanese banks faced the problem of non-performing loans, which were the loans that could not be repaid, and bank lending shrank significantly. In this economic situation, the LDP government, which had been in power since 1955, finally collapsed in 1993, also due to rampant political scandals. After that, the new non-LDP coalition government composed of eight parties was formed. Although this non-LDP government lasted for less than a year, it achieved two significant goals: electoral reform and the beginning of structural reform of the economy. The non-LDP government established a regulatory reform committee and institutionalized a top-down policymaking process for implementing structural reform, which was maintained with some adaptations by the ensuing coalition governments led by the LDP.

The LDP-led coalition government of Prime Minister Hashimoto initiated in the mid-1990s structural reforms targeting the "six burdens" of the economy.[7] Among the most significant reforms was the financial "Big Bang". This financial reform introduced several deregulatory measures such as the liberalization of international capital transactions, fixed brokerage commissions, and financial products such as securities, derivatives and investment trusts (Toya 2006: 120–28). The LDP-led coalition government also introduced market-oriented financial regulatory reform by abandoning the "convoy" system. In the convoy system, big banks were supposed to rescue insolvent small- and medium-sized banks based on administrative guidance issued by the Ministry of Finance (MOF). This was aimed at maintaining the stability of the financial system by not allowing any financial institution to go bankrupt (Brown 1999; Milhaupt 1999; Norville 1998). However, this protective measure made Japanese banks very inefficient. After the collapse of the bubble economy, even big banks were under acute strain due to the deteriorating problem of non-performing loans and were no longer able to rescue insolvent small- and medium-sized banks. To avoid collapse of the financial system that followed the Asian financial crisis in 1997–98, the opposition parties led by the DPJ and the LDP reformers forced the LDP government to intro-duce a more market-oriented and rule-based financial supervisory system that imitated the American system (Amyx 2004; Hall 2007; Hori 2005; Watanabe 2015c). This reform was partly possible because of the opposi-tion control of the House of Councillors, which has power to veto bills and is only slightly less powerful than the House of Representatives.

In addition to the liberalization of financial transactions with Big Bang and the introduction of more market-oriented financial regulation, the LDP-led coalition government deregulated the labour market, although deregulation was implemented mostly in non-regular employment such as temporary agency work and fixed-term contracts. For example, the use of temporary agency work was permitted in almost all sectors only with a few exceptions, such as the manufacturing sector. Before this liberali-zation in 1999, employers could use temporary agency work only for a limited number of occupations (Watanabe 2012, 2014, 2015a). Labour unions led by Rengō (Japanese Trade Union Confederation), the larg-est national union confederation in Japan, opposed the liberalization of temporary agency work and partly succeeded in preventing the LDP-led coalition government from introducing wholesale liberalization. Again, this partial success was possible due to the opposition control of the House of Councillors. Rengō was also partly successful in preventing the LDP-led coalition government from expanding the scope of workers to be covered by working-time deregulation in relation to regular employment (called "discretionary work", in which regular employees' working hours are predetermined and no overtime salary is paid except for work on weekends and holidays and late at night) in cooperation with the DPJ-led opposition parties (Watanabe 2012, 2014, 2015a). The DPJ, a more welfare-oriented party than the LDP and the largest opposition party at that time, received political support from Rengō and opposed deregulation of the labour market. Rengō was able to inform the content of labour market reform, albeit to a small extent, despite the greater power resources of employers and the dominance of the LDP as a pro-business party because Rengō was able to maintain access to the labour policymaking process in government (Watanabe 2012, 2014, 2015a).

KOIZUMI ADMINISTRATION'S REGULATORY REFORMS AND THE NEW GOVERNMENT OF THE DEMOCRATIC PARTY OF JAPAN

The Koizumi administration (2001–06) had implemented structural reform of the economy more extensively than previous LDP administrations. Prime Minister Koizumi is probably most well-known for having privatized post offices, which played a significant political role in mobilizing their employees to vote for the LDP at elections. The stationmasters of post offices maintained close connections with the LDP and led political support groups for the party (called *"kōenkai"*). In the Japanese economy, post offices are also financial institutions, allowing people to deposit money at slightly higher interest rates than those of commercial banks. Post offices were the largest financial institution in Japan in terms of personal savings. Part of this large amount of saved money was used for public works through the Fiscal and Investment Loan Programme (FILP). The FILP was not only an economic but also a political programme, as many public corporations were established to carry out politically oriented public works such as the construction of roads and bridges using FILP money. Many of those public corporations were inefficient and wasted Japanese people's saving money. Also, public corporations were among the main sources of employment for retired bureaucrats (called *"amakudari"*, literally meaning "the descent from heaven"; in this case heaven meant the bureaucracy, which given their power and authority in Japanese politics, were perceived as the elite). In *amakudari*, many former bureaucrats served public corporations as presidents and directors. In addition, public works implemented by public corporations were hotbeds for corruption involving construction companies such as *dangō* (price rigging). Political corruption was rampant in Japanese politics under the 1955 system (Woodall 1996).

Prime Minister Koizumi sought to privatize post offices in order to reduce inefficiency and waste in the national economy. To cut the link between post office savings, the FILP and public corporations, Koizumi reformed the FILP so that it would need to raise funds by issuing bonds instead of simply using post office savings. Koizumi also attempted to privatize other public corporations such as the Japan Highway Public Corporation to make their administration and operation more efficient and less costly. The privatization of post offices met strong political resistance from post office stationmasters, LDP *zoku* politicians with close political links to post offices and the Ministry of Construction. Privatization was a critical issue for those political actors with vested interest to lose, such as station masters (jobs), *zoku* politicians (a reliable political support group) and bureaucrats of the Ministry of Construction (*amakudari*). In order to reduce the influence of these vested interests in the policymaking process and implement postal reform, Koizumi used Cabinet councils such as the Council on Economic and Fiscal Policy, whose membership positions were occupied by neoliberal business leaders and economists who wanted to promote structural reform and achieve greater economic efficiency (Maclachlan 2011: 138–42). The bill to privatize the postal offices was submitted to the Diet in this political process regardless of the strong opposition. When the bill was rejected in the House of Councillors despite marginally passing the House of Representatives, Koizumi dissolved the Diet and withdrew party support for those LDP members who had not backed his privatization bill for the coming election. Instead, he replaced those LDP members with party candidates who supported the bill. The LDP won a landslide victory in the following election to the House of

Representatives and both Houses of the Diet approved his postal privatization bill.

The Koizumi administration also implemented reform in other economic sectors. For example, the labour market was further liberalized, although it was mostly in non-regular employment as in the case of the late 1990s. While temporary agency work was not permitted in the manufacturing sector despite the liberalization of temporary work in 1999, the 2003 amendment to the Temporary Work Agency Law enabled employers to use temporary workers in the manufacturing sector. Given the importance of the sector in the Japanese economy, this amendment was significant. It was partly possible, as the LDP had a majority in both Houses of the Diet. In the case of the 1999 amendment, the opposition parties led by the DPJ controlled the less powerful House of Councillors (Watanabe 2012, 2014, 2015a). In addition to temporary agency work, the use of fixed-term contracts was also further liberalized, and the scope of discretionary work was expanded so that employers would be able to use a larger number of regular workers more flexibly in terms of their working hours. To facilitate labour market reform, the Koizumi administration removed labour representatives from the policymaking process in Cabinet councils such as the Council on Economic and Fiscal Policy and the Regulatory Reform Council. These councils were established to represent business interests to a greater extent and promote structural reform. Although labour unions led by Rengō remained in the policymaking process in the advisory councils of the newly established Ministry of Health, Labour and Welfare (MHLW), Cabinet councils acquired agenda-setting power and the policymaking autonomy of the MHLW's advisory councils was partly undermined (Watanabe 2012, 2014, 2015a). As a result, labour's interests became less well represented in the Koizumi administration.

After the Koizumi administration, the LDP had three short-time administrations between 2006 and 2009, with each administration lasting for only less than a year. As a result, those administrations did not implement significant economic reforms aimed at deregulation. In fact, as a result of the structural reform by the Koizumi administration, especially deregulation of non-regular employment, a "gap" society (*kakusa shakai*), a society with a high degree of inequality and an increasing number of "working poor", became a prominent social issue. The working poor in Japan are often defined as those workers whose annual income is less than ¥2 million (around $18,000 at the exchange rate of $1.00 = ¥110). As a result, structural reform of the economy became a less salient issue after the Koizumi administration, with a few exceptions such as a failed attempt by the first Abe administration to introduce the "white-collar exemption", a deregulatory measure to exempt a certain category of white-collar worker from working-time regulation (Igarashi 2008: 110–20).

Figure 2.1 Japan's GDP quarterly growth rate before and after the 2008 global financial crisis

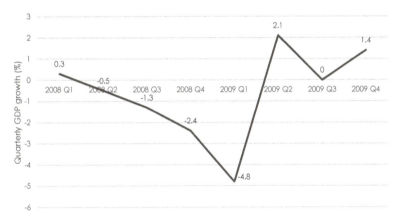

Source: OECD Stat.

When the global financial crisis occurred, the Japanese economy shrank significantly as a result of a massive decrease in exports to the American and European markets, which were originally hit hard by the global financial crisis. Japanese GDP shrank by 9.6 per cent (on an annual basis) in the fourth quarter of 2008 and 19.2 per cent (on an annual basis) in the first quarter of 2009 (see Figure 2.1). In addition to the negative impact of the global financial crisis, the structural reforms implemented by the Koizumi administration had already increased the level of income inequality and the working poor, as mentioned above, which had a negative impact on the LDP's maintenance of power. Against this socio-economic background, the DPJ achieved a landslide victory in the election to the House of Representatives in September 2009. It was the first time Japan experienced a real change of power based on the result of an election since the formation of the LDP in 1955.

The DPJ's election manifesto pledged that it would seek to reduce bureaucracy and strengthen the leadership of the governing party. As for the economy, the DPJ promised to reduce unnecessary public works to increase efficiency in budget spending and instead increase welfare spending such as subsidies for raising children. However, the Japanese economy remained stagnant. A highly appreciated yen, which had a negative impact on Japanese exports, and low stock prices were part of the reasons. Deflation also continued during the DPJ administration. Despite benefitting consumers, deflation negatively affected business because of stagnant wages, low consumer spending and low investment by companies. By the time the DPJ announced its intention to raise consumption tax at odds with what it had announced in its election manifesto in 2010, its popularity was low. The (perceived) mishandling of the 3.11 triple disasters[8] by the administration of Prime Minister Kan also affected the popularity of the DPJ negatively. The DPJ suffered a huge loss in the election to the House of Representatives in 2012 and lost power.

LDP'S RETURN TO POWER AND THE IMPLEMENTATION OF "ABENOMICS"

The LDP came back to power in December 2012. Abe Shinzō, who had been prime minister after Koizumi for less than a year due to the LDP's loss in the election to the House of Councillors in 2007 and his poor health, became prime minister again. Based on his understanding that the failure of his first administration was due to his focus on politically controversial issues such as constitutional change, Prime Minister Abe adopted a survival strategy of economy first and announced the launch of an economic policy entitled "Abenomics". In Abenomics, economic growth is considered the number one priority. However, it can also be considered as an essential tool for the Abe administration to achieve its ultimate goal of constitutional reform by maintaining popular support for the administration with strong economic growth and thus remaining in power.

Abenomics: monetary policy, fiscal policy and structural reform

Abenomics was composed of three "arrows" of "monetary policy", "fiscal policy" and "structural reform". The term "arrows" means the instruments for targeting the goal of economic growth in comparison to "archery", which Prime Minister Abe practiced when he was a university student. Among these three policies, the most significant was monetary policy, which targeted 2 per cent inflation with the BOJ's purchase of government bonds and an increase in the money supply. Fiscal policy was essentially the same as that implemented by previous LDP administrations and was mostly concerned with spending tax money on public works and increasing jobs in the construction and other relevant sectors. Structural reform was aimed at deregulating the economy so that it would be able to make the Japanese economy more efficient. However, with a small number of exceptions, most structural reform measures did not go beyond Abe's rhetoric and turned out to be insufficient.

As for monetary policy, the Abe administration has sought to overcome deflation and achieve economic growth by increasing the monetary base and pursuing an annual inflation rate of 2 per cent. The government policymakers believed (and still believe) that mild inflation would contribute to economic growth by stimulating investment and production, increasing corporate profits and wages, and increasing workers' spending. An increase in the money supply was also aimed at depreciating yen and increasing Japanese exports, although the government has denied seeking to devalue its currency in response to criticisms from some countries, especially the United States under the Trump administration. Cheaper yen also tends to raise stock prices, as investors tend to think it will increase Japanese companies' exports and profits.

The BOJ had been traditionally "conservative" (or "hawkish") about government spending. It was especially hesitant to purchase government bonds. However, the new BOJ Governor Kuroda Haruhiko, appointed by Prime Minister Abe, shares Abe's belief that Japan needs to end deflation to achieve economic growth. As an economic scholar who believes in "reflation", which is aimed at introducing inflation by the government monetary policy to stimulate the economy, Kuroda has implemented a policy of "quantitative easing", aimed at increasing money supply through the BOJ's purchase of government bonds, corporate bonds and stocks. The BOJ has also been involved in the purchase of exchange-traded fund (ETF) mainly for the purpose of maintaining stock prices. Along with ETF, the government has used the Government Pension Investment Fund (GPIF) to invest pension money to purchase government bonds and stocks. Stock prices are among the most important economic indicators for the Abe administration, as they are used as a metric for showing how well Abenomics is performing.

As for fiscal policy, the Abe administration increased the amount of government spending on public works to stimulate the economy. In addition to traditional public works with a political purpose of providing jobs to construction companies as the LDP's loyal supporters, the government also aimed to renovate old infrastructure. As a result of a large amount of continued spending on public works, the public debt of Japanese national and local governments exceeded 250 per cent in 2017, which was by far the largest among OECD countries. The two-time postponing of a consumption tax hike planned in October 2015 and April 2017 also exacerbated the fiscal condition of the Japanese government as it was planned to finance social welfare spending. However, the Abe administration postponed it twice for fear of a negative impact on economic growth. As a result, neither public debt or the government deficit has decreased, and the Japanese government has not been able to achieve its target of running a primary balance surplus. There is a lack of fiscal discipline in Abenomics, as its primary purpose is economic growth rather than a balanced budget.

The Abe administration has sought to promote structural reform in order to make the economy more efficient and achieve economic growth. Prime Minister Abe declared in 2013 that his administration would transform Japan into the country that has the "best" environment in the world for foreign companies to do business, despite the fact that Japan's inward FDI (per cent of GDP) was only 3.7 per cent, compared to the UK's 51.5 per cent, the US's 16.9 per cent and Korea's 12.6 per cent as of the end of 2011. The Abe administration selected as priority areas for deregulation such economic sectors as employment, healthcare and agriculture, which were well known for the existence of powerful vested interests that opposed reform. In order to implement these structural reforms in a speedy, top-down manner, the administration introduced several changes in policymaking, for example, the establishment of new Cabinet councils such as the Industrial Competitiveness Council as well as reviving several previous Cabinet councils, which were in hiatus during the former DPJ administration, such as the Council on Economic and Fiscal Policy and the Regulatory Reform Council (Watanabe 2018a). However, these Cabinet councils discussed similar policy issues simultaneously and were inefficient in policymaking. In addition, their attitudes toward structural reform were not necessarily the same because of the different memberships of those Cabinet councils. For example, while the Industrial Competitiveness Council and the Regulatory Reform Council have been pro-deregulation and proposed radical reforms (in the Japanese standard), the Council on Economic and Fiscal Policy has been more cautious and ambivalent about radical reform and preferred more restrained reform. In addition, different opinions exist on the degree and content of deregulation even within each Cabinet council.

As mentioned above, the Abe administration proposed reforming several economic sectors, including employment, healthcare and agriculture. As for employment, the administration proposed policy measures aimed at increasing flexibility of the labour market. In order to promote the transfer of workers from declining to growing economic sectors, Cabinet councils such as the Industrial Competitiveness Council proposed introducing fiduciary compensation in the case of unfair dismissal to reduce the rigid employment protection of regular workers. The government claimed that the reduced uncertainties for employers involving labour disputes at the time of dismissal would increase employment of regular workers. In addition, Cabinet councils proposed increasing the number of so-called "semi-regular" workers, who are regular workers in status but their working time, work locations and job responsibilities are limited, in contrast to those of "ordinary" regular workers under lifetime employment (Watanabe 2018a). Semi-regular work was introduced to promote work-life balance and increase the number of female workers so that a greater labour input of female workers would contribute to economic growth. Among the controversial measures along with the fiduciary compensation for unfair dismissal was working-time deregulation in relation to regular employment. The Abe administration proposed introducing the category of "highly professional work", which would be exempt from working-time regulation and not entitled to overtime pay under any circumstances unlike "discretionary work". The salaries of workers under highly professional work are pre-determined as in the case of discretionary work. However, discretionary work only partly exempts a certain category of regular workers from working-time regulation and those employees under discretionary work are still entitled to overtime pay for the work conducted on weekends, holidays and late at night. The government claimed that the introduction of highly professional work as well as the expansion of discretionary work would improve labour productivity and contribute to economic growth.

The Abe administration also deregulated non-regular employment. For example, the administration enabled employers to use temp workers for the same jobs without time limit, which was enacted as the 2015 amendment to the Temporary Agency Work Law. The administration also proposed tax reforms to abolish the gender-based treatment that favoured families with full-time housewives and low-income mothers in part-time work. Previously, workers (almost always women) whose annual income was less than ¥1.03 million (a little more than $9,000) were exempted from paying income tax and their spouse (almost always husbands) were also entitled to an income tax deduction. The initiative was aimed at encouraging women to work for longer hours so that the government would be able to reduce labour shortage and promote economic growth with their greater spending power as a result of their higher income. However, this proposal failed to materialize, as the LDP government gave it up in fear of voter backlash from families with full-time housewives and low-income female part-time workers. Instead, the Abe administration decided to raise the annual income ceiling for exemption from income tax from ¥1.03 million yen to ¥1.5 million. However, this was a far cry from the original proposal aimed at eliminating a gender-based tax system and promoting women's labour market participation. In addition, other gender-based arrangements such as the payment for social insurance and corporate fringe benefits remained the same. In the case of social insurance, (female) workers whose annual income is less than ¥1.3 million do not need to pay a premium for pension and health insurance as they are covered by their husband's pension and health insurance programs. Corporate fringe benefits such as family allowance have similar arrangements based on gender division of labour, and only workers with a spouse (almost always women) in a low annual income of ¥1.03 million or lower are entitled to those corporate fringe benefits.

In addition to employment reform, the Abe administration sought to increase the competitiveness of Japanese agriculture by abolishing the guidance and auditing functions of the JA-Zenchū (Japanese Central Union of Agricultural Cooperatives) and allowing individual farmers to have greater autonomy in agricultural business. This measure was also aimed at preparing Japanese agriculture for trade liberalization such as participation in the Trans-Pacific Partnership (Ito 2015; Kujiraoka 2016: 102–11; Nishikawa 2017). The Abe administration also proposed to introduce a new corporate governance code, which included auditing by external directors so that Japanese companies could make their business more efficient and productive. In addition, the administration proposed to decrease corporate tax from around 35 per cent to less than 30 per cent (see Figure 3.9 in Chapter 3).

The Abe administration established "strategic special zones" (*"senryaku tokku"*) as a measure to promote the structural reform of the economy. Japan has more than 14,000 regulatory laws and government and ministerial ordinances, and some of them have been obstacles to an efficient and productive economy based on free market principles. The government established these strategic special zones as exceptional areas where some of these laws and ordinances would not be enforced and companies would be able to enjoy some deregulatory measures without which they would not be able to pursue their business. In addition to proposing employment policy measures aimed at increasing the flexibility of the labour market such as easier dismissal, the Abe administration proposed measures to permit the use of foreign workers as housemaids and day-care workers, to permit private companies to own more than 50 per cent of the shares of agricultural businesses, and the promotion of business venture start-ups in the strategic special zones. The government designated the metropolitan areas of Tokyo and Osaka, one prefecture (Okinawa) and three cities as strategic special zones for the first time, with the Tokyo metropolitan area aimed at attracting foreign companies; the Osaka metropolitan area aimed at innovating medical industry; Okinawa prefecture aimed at promoting tourism with a relaxation of visa regulations; Fukuoka city aimed at attracting business ventures and start-ups (although it is difficult to predict to what extent the permission to run cafés on the street can be an effective deregulatory measure to promote new business ventures); and a city in Hyōgo prefecture and the Nīgata city aimed at reforming agricultural business by promoting innovative, large-scale farming.

Abenomics as the growth strategy of the Abe administration achieved some positive results within a few years of its implementation, at least from the government perspective. For example, monetary policy (the first arrow of Abenomics) based on quantitative easing depreciated Japanese yen and, with greater expectation by investors of more exports by Japanese companies, stock prices went up. Japanese companies, especially larger ones, achieved a record amount of profits. The unemployment rate also decreased, although most newly created jobs were non-regular work. However, the government could not achieve its annual inflation target of 2 per cent to escape from deflation and the wage growth remained stagnant overall. BOJ Governor Kuroda subscribed to the "inflation expectation" theory: the belief that people who expect inflation (due to the increase in money supply) are inclined to spend money before prices go up. However, he (and many economists who have an unrealistic understanding of the real economy) did not appreciate that people who are less affluent or cannot afford to spend more money tend to save money to prepare for the future, rather than spend, even in the situation of increased money supply. This behaviour of Japanese consumers has been recognized for a long time, but Kuroda has failed to understand it, partly because he does not want to admit his policy of quantitative easing has been ineffective and failed to achieve "reflation".

Economic growth remained low (GDP growth of around 1 per cent on average) despite the creation of many public works based on the second arrow of fiscal policy. Although the third arrow of structural reform was considered to have long-term positive effects on economic growth, in contrast to the short-term positive effects of monetary and fiscal policies, the implementation of the structural reforms by the Abe administration was mostly insufficient, especially from the perspective of economic growth. This was largely due to the opposition by bureaucrats, LDP *zoku* politicians and protected business with vested interests. For bureaucrats, regulations are the tools to maintain their power. Protected business has been the reliable supporters of the LDP at the time of elections, and the LDP *zoku* politicians with strong links with protected business in their policy areas have opposed the structural reforms so that they would be able to survive elections. Also, the Abe administration was unable to implement structural reforms because of fear of their unpopularity and the consequences for them at the next election. In addition, due to a lack of the capacity and strong leadership of Prime Minister Abe, the structural reforms were not implemented enough to promote economic growth, despite his rhetoric.

New Abenomics

Abenomics was only partially successful at best. As a result, Prime Minister Abe announced "new" Abenomics in September 2015, more than two and a half years after the inauguration of his second administration in December 2012. New Abenomics comprised three new arrows. The first new arrow was the combination of the old three arrows of Abenomics: monetary policy based on quantitative easing, fiscal policy based on a large amount of public works spending, and the structural reform of the economy. It was summarized as a growth strategy aimed at a GDP of ¥600 trillion. The new second arrow was aimed at increasing the country's low fertility rate from around 1.4 (children per woman) to 1.8. The third arrow sought to address the problem of workers leaving the workforce in order to look after elderly parents.

In new Abenomics, he claimed to create a "society in which all 100 million people can be active". However, Prime Minister Abe's proposals in new Abenomics were unrealistic. For example, the Japanese economy would need to grow at an annual rate of 3 per cent to achieve GDP of ¥600 trillion by 2020. The Abe administration had never achieved such a high growth rate. Japan's fertility rate improved only to a very small extent but has recently begun to fall again. Due to the difficulty of striking a work-life balance and a shortage of childcare centers, it is unrealistic to expect the fertility rate to grow to 1.8 in the near future. Even with an increased number of daycare centers, the number of daycare providers is insufficient – the combination of low wages and very hard work make it an unattractive sector. Similarly, the shortage of care workers for the elderly means the task of caring for the elderly parents remains with their children. As usual, numerous Cabinet councils and ministries were involved in the "all-active" plan and the policy-making process has become unduly complicated. In fact, ministries have taken advantage of the all-active plan to acquire a greater amount of fiscal budget to implement their own pet projects. A lack of coordination among ministries and Cabinet councils is likely to result in insufficient achievements of new Abenomics. In addition, the lack of fiscal discipline is likely to aggravate Japan's already heavy public debt even further.

Despite less emphasis on structural reforms in new Abenomics, economic growth through higher labour productivity remains a core economic policy of the Abe administration. For example, the administration aimed to introduce the "Work-Style Reform" to enhance labour productivity and achieve economic growth. The Work-Style Reform bill passed in the Diet and became law in June 2018. The Work-Style Reform combined both worker-protection and neoliberal deregulatory measures, as seen in the combination of reduction of overtime work and the introduction of "equal pay for equal work" (worker-protection measures) and the introduction of the category of "highly professional work" and the expansion of discretionary work (neoliberal deregulatory measures). Excessive amount of overtime work, which has caused a large number of deaths due to over-work (called "*karōshi*" in Japanese), remains a big problem in Japan. To cope with this problem, the government has stipulated the maximum hours of overtime work with penalties for violations. "Equal pay for equal work" is aimed at improving the working conditions of non-regular workers such as part-time and temporary workers, but the government also sought to increase the spending power of non-regular workers and thus promote economic growth. The introduction of highly professional work and the expansion of discretionary work (later abandoned) are working-time deregulatory measures aimed at both enhancing labour productivity of regular workers and reducing the amount of overtime pay.

As for other employment and labour market reform measures, the Abe administration enacted an amendment to the law on technical internship to facilitate the increase in the number of technical interns from foreign countries. As they are not classified as workers and their protection by the Labour Standards Law and other labour laws is limited, their working conditions are extremely poor and precarious. For this very reason, however, the use of technical interns has been very popular among employers in such sectors as construction and agriculture that have suffered from labour shortages.

As the number of technical interns was not large enough to fill labour demand, however, the Abe administration announced their intention to create an official route to low-skilled employment in order to increase the number of foreign workers for such employment. In December 2018, the Abe administration enacted a law amending the Immigration Control Law that officially permitted immigration of (relatively) low-skilled workers. The new immigration visa called "designated" or "specified" skills (*tokutei ginō*) composed two categories. The first category is for migrant workers with a certain level of (low) skill and was introduced in April 2019 to 14 industrial sectors that have suffered from labour shortages such as elderly care, construction and agriculture. Migrant workers in this category can stay in Japan up to five years but these years are not counted towards the ten-year stay required to apply for permanent residency. They are also not allowed to bring family members to Japan. The second category is for migrant workers with a higher level of skills than those of the first category workers, which are assessed by government-sponsored exams implemented in collaboration with the relevant industrial associations. In contrast to the first category, the number of years of their stay in Japan is counted towards those required to apply for permanent residency. Migrant workers in the second category can also bring family members to Japan.

The number of migrant workers in the second category is unlikely to be large given the strict immigration criteria, so it is expected that the majority of workers arriving under this new visa will be in the first category. In addition, close to 50 per cent of migrant worker visas in the first category are expected to be taken up by the current technical interns who would be transferred from the existing technical intern category. Given the requirement not to bring in family members and the impossibility to apply for permanent residency in the first category and the strict criteria of the second category, it is not clear whether this new immigration visa will be able to meet the labour shortage. In addition, Japan needs to compete for labour migrants with other countries in East Asia such as South

Korea and Taiwan, which also suffer from labour shortages. Japan's new visa for low-skilled workers is unlikely to be attractive enough for migrant workers, which is perhaps unsurprising given Prime Minister Abe's need to emphasize that the measure was restrictive and not aimed at mass immigration. The Abe administration has relied on the political support of conservative voters and the new visa is an attempt to strike a balance between economic growth policy and conservative immigration policy.

Achievements and problems of Abenomics

The Abe administration has implemented its signature economic policy "Abenomics", both old and new, for almost seven years (as of February 2020). To what extent has Abenomics contributed (or not) to economic growth? Although the monetary policy based on quantitative easing was successful at depreciating the yen and increasing the profits of export-oriented companies, the BOJ has not yet been able to achieve the 2 per cent annual inflation target. In addition, the BOJ's purchase of a huge amount of government bonds and company shares, along with the purchase of the GPIF, has distorted the sound operation of the bond and stock markets. The BOJ's recent change in monetary policy by introducing negative interest rates has also caused problems for the operation of financial institutions such as banks, insurance companies and pension funds by reducing their profits. Should bond prices drop significantly and bond rates increase rapidly, that would not only undermine the financial health of the BOJ and increase government debt, but it also has the potential to severely damage the Japanese economy. In addition to the potential hazard that could be caused by monetary policy, the fiscal policy of Abenomics has discouraged the government to attend to the issue of balancing the budget and has increased the already large amount of government debt. The slight increase in tax revenues brought about by economic growth through Abenomics has been too small to reduce the government debt to any significant extent. Prime Minister Abe's reluctance to cut government spending and his postponement of raising the rate of consumption tax twice in the past has led to a lack of fiscal discipline.

In addition to the monetary and fiscal policies of Abenomics having become less effective in achieving economic growth and even detrimental to the health of the Japanese economy, the structural reforms as a long-term solution to the stagnant economy have not been sufficiently implemented. As mentioned above, despite its rhetoric, electoral concerns have discouraged the Abe administration from combatting vested interests. Also, the existence of different opinions on how to promote the structural reforms in Cabinet councils has prevented the Abe administration from implementing the reform in a coordinated manner. There have been battles in Cabinet councils between neoliberals, who propose deregulation of the economy and a smaller government, and METI bureaucrats, who rely on industrial policy aimed at investing government money in economic sectors identified as strategic. While the Abe administration has implemented a number of neoliberal policies, such as the introduction of the highly professional work and the further liberalization of temporary agency work, Abenomics retains the quintessential "industrial policy", which sees government intervening in the economy and instructing private companies to engage in its desired economic activities, as in its requests for companies to invest more money in the domestic market and raise wages to achieve economic growth. This dual characteristics of Abenomics may reflect the membership of Cabinet councils, which includes both neoliberals and interventionists, but it also reflects Prime Minister Abe's inheritance of his grandfather and former Prime Minister Kishi's socio-economic ideology of state intervention and big government. Prime Minister Abe seeks to achieve economic growth irrespective of whether they are neoliberal or Keynesian measures. However, partly as a result of the insufficient implementation of the structural reforms of the highly regulated economy, whether by the government or private business associations, Abenomics has been unsuccessful in many respects and Japan's economic efficiency and labour productivity remain low, especially in the service sectors.

3

Measuring the Japanese economy

This chapter will measure the Japanese economy. The chapter will examine data on GDP, prices and productivity in the first section, the foreign sector such as trade (exports and imports) and FDI in the second section, and the public sector such as government expenditures and revenues, taxes, government deficits and public debts in the third section. In the final section, the chapter will analyze the welfare state in terms of social welfare services, including state pension provision, healthcare, elderly (long-term) care and unemployment insurance, and the socioeconomic situation in Japan related to welfare services such as inequality, poverty and an aging population. Other population-related issues such as fertility rates and regional disparities in population will be examined in Chapter 5.

GDP, PRICES AND PRODUCTIVITY

Japan's gross domestic product (GDP) was around $4.971 trillion as of 2018 according to the World Bank data and is the third largest in the world (after the United States and China). Since the collapse of the bubble economy in the early 1990s, Japan's GDP growth has been stagnant. Its GDP in Japanese Yen was around ¥533 trillion in 1997 just before the outbreak of the Asian financial crisis and its own subsequent financial crisis.

Since then, Japan's GDP fell below the level of 1997 and it was only in 2015 that it recovered to the level of 1997. After the global financial crisis in 2007–08, Japan's GDP dropped below ¥500 trillion. Negative growth can be seen in several years, including in 1998 (-1.1%) and 1999 (-0.3%) soon after the Asian financial crisis, and in 2008 (-1.1%) and 2009 (-5.4%) after the global financial crisis (see Figure 3.1).

Figure 3.1 Japan's GDP growth, 1997–2015

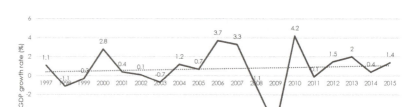

Source: World Bank (2017).

Although the size of Japan's GDP was about eight times as large as China's in the 1990s (see Figure 3.2), the difference shrank to around four times in 2000 and around twice in 2005. China's GDP surpassed Japan's in 2010, growing to more than twice the size by 2015. Compared to the GDP of the US, Japan's was around one-third or half before 1995, when the gap shrank to about 50 per cent. However, this was at least partly due to the highly appreciated Japanese yen against the US dollar. Since then, the gap widened, and the GDP of the US had reached around four times that of Japan's in 2015. This is also partly due to the relatively depreciated Japanese yen against the dollar.

Japan has experienced periods of deflation since the collapse of the bubble economy in the early 1990s. When we measure inflation and deflation based on the core consumer price index (core CPI: total minus food and energy, annual growth percentage) between 2011 and 2017, Japan experienced deflation in 2011, 2012 and 2013 (-0.75%, -0.49%, -0.09%

respectively) but inflation in 2014, 2015 and 2016 (1.98%, 1.02% and 0.4% respectively). However, the core CPI index became negative (-0.07%) in 2017 and Japan again experienced deflation (see Figure 3.3). It seems that Abenomics contributed to Japan's escape from deflation sometimes but not always.

Figure 3.2 Japan, China and US GDP, 1985–2015

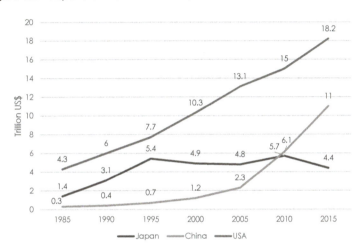

Source: World Bank (2017).

Japan's labour productivity measured in GDP per hours worked is low compared to many countries and is the lowest among the G7 (see Figure 3.4). While the GDP per hour worked of the US was $64.2 in 2017, Japan's was $41.8, which was less than two-thirds of the United States. The growth of labour productivity in Japan was also low at 0.4 per cent between 2000 and 2017 (Nihon Keizai Shimbun 2019a). The reasons for Japan's low labour productivity will be examined in Chapter 6, but one major reason is inefficiency in the economy due to a lack of online digitalization, which can be partly explained by government regulation and the self-regulation in industries.

Figure 3.3 Japan's inflation (CPI less food and energy), 2011–17

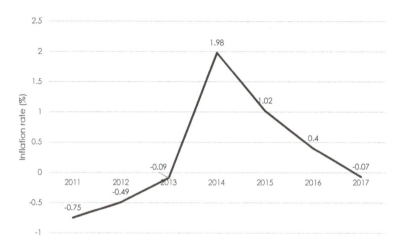

Source: OECD (2019).

Figure 3.4 Labour productivity of G7 countries, 2017

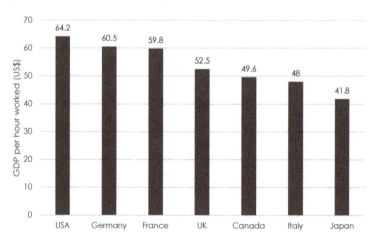

Source: OECD (2019).

FOREIGN SECTOR

Table 3.1 shows Japan's exports and imports in time-series data since 1950 at five-year intervals plus 2008 and 2009 (years of the global financial crisis) and 2014 (when Japan had the largest trade deficit). According to the Ministry of Finance, Japan had trade deficits in the early years after the Second World War (1950–63) but then mostly a trade surplus until 2010 except in a few years, most notably around the time of the oil crises in the 1970s. Since 2011, however, Japan has had trade deficits, except in 2016 and 2017. The highly appreciated yen after the global financial crisis in 2008 accelerated the pace of moving production facilities overseas by several Japanese firms, which contributed to Japan's trade deficits due to the smaller amounts of Japanese exports and the increased amounts of imports from Japanese subsidiaries overseas. This also negatively affected the profits of Japanese SMEs that produced the components for large Japanese manufacturing companies. Ever intensifying competition from neighbouring Asian countries further contributed to Japan's trade deficits. In 2014, Japan had its largest trade deficits of around ¥13 trillion.

Table 3.1 Japan's exports and imports, 1950–2015 (billion ¥)

Year	Exports	Imports	Year	Exports	Imports
1950	298.0	348.2	1995	41,530.9	31,548.8
1955	723.8	889.7	2000	51,654.2	40,938.4
1960	1,459.6	1,616.8	2005	65,656.5	56,949.4
1965	3,042.6	2,940.8	2008	81,018.1	78,954.7
1970	6,954.4	6,797.2	2009	54,170.6	51,499.4
1975	16,545.3	17,170.1	2010	67,399.6	60,765.0
1980	29,382.5	31,995.3	2014	73,093.0	85,909.1
1985	41,955.7	31,084.9	2015	75,613.9	78,405.5
1990	41,456.9	33,855.2			

Source: Ministry of Finance 2019.

Table 3.2 shows Japan's exports and imports in goods in 2018. Japan had a trade deficit in goods of around $10 billion in 2018 – a trend first identified in the 2010s. Japan had a trade surplus towards East Asia (China, South Korea, Taiwan, Hong Kong and ASEAN) as a whole but on an individual country basis, had trade deficits with China (around $30 billion). Japan had the largest trade surplus by country with the United States at around $60 billion. Japan had trade deficits of $4.5 billion with the European Union, but its largest trade deficit of around $70 billion was with the Middle East, from where Japan imports a large amount of oil and liquefied natural gas. Japan's balance of payments on current account has been in surplus and it recorded the current account surplus of around $175 billion in 2018.

Table 3.2 Japan's exports and imports in goods by area and country, 2018 (US$ billion)

Area/country	Exports	Imports	Balance
TOTAL	737.8	748.1	-10.3
East Asia	387.8	347.1	40.8
China	143.9	173.5	-29.6
Korea	52.5	32.1	20.3
ASEAN	114.4	112.2	2.2
USA	140.0	81.5	58.5
EU	83.4	87.9	-4.5
Middle East	22.1	93.8	-71.8

Source: JETRO 2019.
Note: East Asia includes China, South Korea, Taiwan, Hong Kong and ASEAN.

Japan's outward foreign direct investment (FDI) (flow and net) has been much larger than its inward FDI (flow and net). While Japan's outward FDI increased significantly from around $22.7 billion in 1995 to around $138.4 billion in 2015 (in the most recently available data, $159.1 billion in 2018), the amount of Japan's inward FDI has fluctuated at a low level since 1995, when the amount was only $40 million (see Tables 3.3 and 3.4). While the amount of Japan's inward FDI was around $8.2 billion in 2000, it decreased to around $3.2 billion in 2005, and the net amount became negative in 2010 (outflow from Japan by around $1.4 billion more than inflow) before it became positive again in 2015 (around $5.3 billion; and in the most recently available data, $25.9 billion in 2018). However, this amount of Japan's inward FDI in 2015 is less than 4 per cent of Japan's outward FDI in the same year. The existence of *keiretsu* and the regulations by the government and industrial associations are among the main reasons for the small amount of Japan's inward FDI, as we shall see in Chapter 4. By country, the United States has been the largest destination for Japan's outward FDI. In 2015, Japan's outward FDI in the US was a little more than $50 billion, in the EU $35 billion and in China $10 billion (see Table 3.3). As for Japan's inward FDI, the United States provided the largest amount in 2015 (on net basis). However, the amount (around $4.3 billion) was less than 10 per cent of Japanese investment in the US in the same year. The EU was also a large investor in Japan but withdrew more than it invested in 2015 with a negative investment of more than $2 billion (see Table 3.4).

Table 3.3 Japan's outward FDI (net and flow, US$ million), 1995–2015

	1995	2000	2005	2010	2015
China	3,183	934	6,575	7,252	10,011
Korea	347	1,074	1,736	1,085	1,593
ASEAN	3,987	207	5,032	8,930	20,920
USA	9,018	14,121	12,126	9,193	50,218
EU	3,230	10,968	7,872	8,359	35,785
World	22,651	31,534	45,461	57,223	138,428

Source: JETRO 2019.

Table 3.4   Japan's inward FDI (net and flow, US$ million), 1995–2015

	1995	2000	2005	2010	2015
China	-22	0	11	314	636
Korea	117	48	31	274	932
ASEAN	6	76	592	1,810	2,324
USA	294	-1,052	308	2,961	4,338
EU	84	3,913	1,858	132	-2,104
World	40	8,226	3,223	-1,359	5,253

Source: JETRO 2019.

In terms of FDI stock, which measures the total level of FDI at a given point of time, Japan's outward FDI in stock in the whole world was a little more than $1.2 trillion in 2015. However, Japan's inward FDI in stock was only a little more than $200 billion, as to be expected given the small amount of FDI inflow to Japan. The largest destination of Japan's FDI in stock was the US ($400 billion in 2015) while Japan's FDI in stock in China and EU were around $109 billion and around $291 billion respectively. The European Union was the largest investor in Japan in terms of stock in the amount of around $87 billion in 2015. The US was the second, with an accumulated investment in Japan of around $57 billion.

Finally, Japan has been one of the largest creditor countries of foreign exchange reserves in the world. Japan's foreign exchange reserves in 2018 was around $1.2 trillion and was only smaller than China's at around $3 trillion. With a large amount of foreign exchange reserves, Japan as well as China may be able to exert certain influence on the political and economic behaviours of debtor countries such as the US.

GOVERNMENT SECTOR

The amounts of the annual expenditures by the Japanese government (general account) have been around ¥100 trillion (around $900 billion at current rates) since the global financial crisis in 2008. The government's largest expenditure in 2018 was ¥33 trillion on social welfare (33.7% of total expenditures), followed by ¥23.3 trillion for government bonds (23.8%), ¥15.5 trillion for subsidies for local government (15.9%) and ¥6 trillion for public works (6.1%) (see Figure 3.5).

Figure 3.5 Composition of the central government's budget on expenditures, general account, 2018

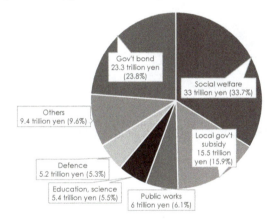

Source: Ministry of Finance, *Fiscal Documents of Japan* (2018).

As for changes in government expenditure, the central government's spending on social welfare (such as pension and healthcare) saw the largest increase (by ¥21.4 trillion from ¥11.6 trillion to ¥33 trillion) between 1990 and 2018 (see Figure 3.6) with the second largest in payments for government bonds (by ¥9 trillion from ¥14.3 trillion to ¥23.3 trillion). As for central government's subsidies to local government, many local governments cannot survive by collecting their own taxes but depend on subsidies from the central government (¥15.5 trillion in 2018). In 2015, for example, local government received only around ¥40 trillion (38.4% of the total revenues of ¥101.9 trillion) through local taxes and a further ¥10.7 trillion (10.5%) by issuing local government bonds. Japanese local government depended on subsidies and other financial support from the central government significantly (around 35% of the total revenues) and this provided the central government with a useful tool to control the activities of local governments.

Figure 3.6 Government expenditures, general account, 1990 and 2018 (¥ trillion)

Source: Ministry of Finance, *Fiscal Documents of Japan* (2019).

There are more than 500,000 construction companies in Japan. The LDP has remained in power by providing construction companies with public works and by receiving votes and donations in return. Public works are a good example of interest group politics in Japan and the LDP has used public works to gain political benefits, particularly since the 1970s when Prime Minister Tanaka himself was a well-known construction *zoku* (policy tribe) politician (Woodall 1996). Although the government's spending on public works has been restrained to some extent since the Koizumi administration implemented the structural reforms of the economy in the early 2000s, Japan's spending on public works is still large in international comparison (see Figure 3.7 on the ratio of gross fixed capital formation – infrastructure investment – to GDP).

Figure 3.7 Gross fixed capital formation (percentage of GDP), 1990–2015

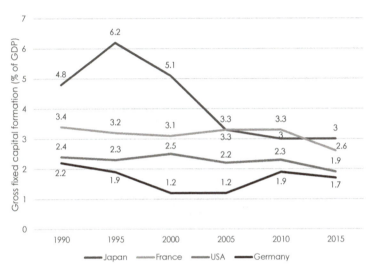

Source: Ministry of Finance, *Fiscal Documents of Japan* (2019).

The fifth and sixth largest areas of government expenditure were "education and science" and "defence". Government spending on education is among the smallest in international comparison: 3.2 per cent of GDP in 2014, which was almost half of Denmark's 6.3 per cent. Most administrations have kept the defence budget at less than 1 per cent of GDP according to Article 9 of the Constitution, which bans Japan from possessing a military. Although the current Abe administration is not constrained by this norm and Japan's defence budget has been the largest under his administration, the ratio of less than 1 per cent of GDP has been maintained due to the increase in Japan's GDP.

As for government revenues, 50 per cent came from the following taxes: income tax (19.5%), consumption tax (18%) and corporate tax

(12.5%) in 2018. Apart from taxes, the Japanese government acquired 34.4 per cent of its revenues by issuing government bonds: special bonds (or deficit bonds) (28.2%) and construction bonds (6.2%) used for implementing public works as the name suggests (see Figure 3.8).

Figure 3.8 Composition of the central government's budget on revenues, general account, 2018

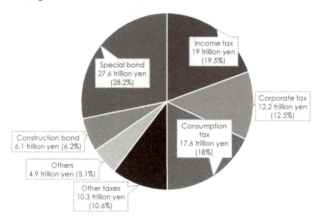

Source: Ministry of Finance, *Fiscal Documents of Japan* (2018).

The composition of taxes and bonds that make up government revenues has changed in the following way. From 1980 until 1990, the gap between tax revenues and the revenues from bond issues was expanding (tax revenues increased from ¥13.8 trillion to ¥60.1 trillion between 1980 and 1990 while the revenues from bond issues decreased from ¥14.2 trillion to ¥6.3 trillion in the same period, partly because of Japan's good economic performance, especially during the bubble economy in the late 1980s). Between 1990 and 2010, the so-called "two lost decades", tax revenues were in a declining trend while the revenues from bond issues were in an increasing trend. In 2015, however, tax revenues increased and the revenues from bond issues decreased in comparison to the level in 2010, given the poor economic performance of the Japanese economy in 2010 and the relatively good economic performance under Abenomics in 2015.

As for the tax composition of government revenues, those through income tax were in a declining trend from 1990 until 2010 but were in an increasing trend between 2010 and 2015. A similar trend can be seen in government revenues from corporate tax. In contrast, the government revenues through consumption tax has been in an increasing trend except in the period between 2005 and 2010, most likely due to the global financial crisis and the resulting slump in consumption. Around 35 per cent of government revenues (central and local) were received through consumption tax in 2018. The next largest source was income tax (around 31%). In international comparison, similar trends can be seen in the tax sources of government revenues in France and Germany. Whereas, in the United States and Sweden, for example, the largest tax source for government revenues was income tax and then consumption tax (sales tax in the US and value added tax in Sweden).

In 2018, Japan's highest rate of income tax – 45 per cent – was the same as that in the UK, Germany and France (37% in the US). However, the lowest rates varied: 0 per cent in Germany and France, 5 per cent in Japan, 10 per cent in the US and 20 per cent in the UK. As for the corporate effective tax rate, it was lowered from 37 per cent to 29.74 per cent in 2018, principally due to the current Abe administration's aim of attracting a larger amount of foreign investment (see Figure 3.9). Japan's current corporate tax rate is lower than France's (33.33%), is similar to the German rate (29.83%) and is slightly higher than the US rate (27.98%). However, the rate in the UK is much lower (19%). Since October 2019, Japan's consumption tax rate or value added tax rate has been 10 per cent (Taiwan 5%; Korea 10%), which is much lower than European rates (typically around 20% but Swedish rate was even higher at 25%).

As seen in Figure 3.8, the Japanese government relied on the issue of government bonds (special, or deficit, bonds and construction bonds) for 34.4 per cent of its total revenues in 2018. Japan has recorded fiscal deficits every year recently and its ratio of fiscal deficits (fiscal balance/GDP) in 2010 after the global financial crisis was -8.1 per cent. This ratio was lower than those of the US and the UK (-12.6% and -9.5% respectively) but was

Figure 3.9 Corporate effective tax rate (%), selected countries, 2018

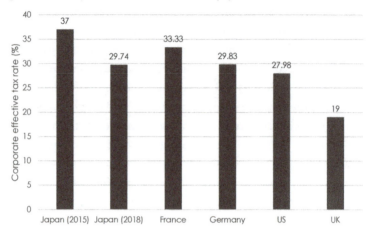

Source: Ministry of Finance (2019).

Note: Japanese data includes 2015 and 2018; other countries are 2018.

Figure 3.10 General government debt, selected countries, percentage of GDP, 2015

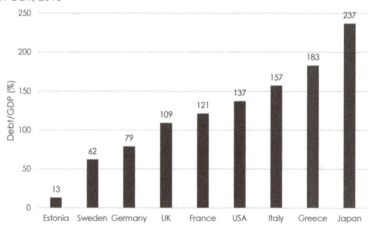

Source: OECD (2019).

higher than those of France, Canada, Italy and Germany (-6.9%, -4.7%, -4.2% and -4.2% respectively).

Japan has accumulated public debts since the government issued its first deficit bond in the 1970s. Although the government's long-term debt as a percentage of GDP was only 10 per cent in 1970, it was 193 per cent in 2015. Its general government debt as a percentage of GDP was 237 per cent in 2015 and was the highest among OECD countries (see Figure 3.10). While most debts are owed to Japanese creditors such as Japanese banks and insurance companies and there is less risk of default by the Japanese government unlike the case of Greece where most debts are owed to foreign creditors, another bad economic situation could cause the selling of government bonds by Japanese creditors and result in the collapse of the bond value and a dramatic rise in interest rates. This would hurt the government's financial health significantly.

WELFARE STATE

Government expenditure on social welfare has expanded dramatically. In 1980, the expenditures on social welfare were around ¥25 trillion, but they had risen to around ¥105 trillion by 2010. In 2018, they were around ¥120 trillion (see Figure 3.11). In 1980, healthcare was the largest social welfare item for government spending (¥10.7 trillion) and pensions was the second largest (at ¥10.5 trillion). However, this situation has since reversed. The largest social welfare item for government spending in 2018 was pensions (¥56.7 trillion) and healthcare was the second (¥39.2 trillion). Other social welfare items accounted for ¥25.3 trillion yen in 2018 with long-term care for the elderly the largest among them (¥10.7 trillion). Japanese expenditures on social welfare as a percentage of GDP was slightly above the OECD average in 2018. While the OECD average was 20.1 per cent, Japan's was 21.9 per cent – higher than Korea (11.1%), the US (18.7%) and the UK (20.6%) but lower than Germany (25.1%), Sweden (26.1%), Italy (27.9%) and France (31.2%).

As noted, government spending on pensions has expanded rapidly.

As a percentage of GDP, it was 9.4 per cent in 2017 and higher than the OECD average (7.5%). It was higher than Anglo-American and other East Asian countries such as Korea (3%), the UK (6.2%) and the US (7.1%), but it was lower than those of continental European countries such as Germany (10.1%), France (13.9%), Italy (16.2%) and Greece (16.9%) (see Figure 3.12). Japan's relatively high percentage is partly due to the aging population and an increase in retired workers. As Japan expects a further increase in its elderly population, the government spending on pensions is likely to increase further but it would be more difficult to sustain the current level of pension.

Figure 3.11   Japanese government's expenditures on social welfare, 1980–2018

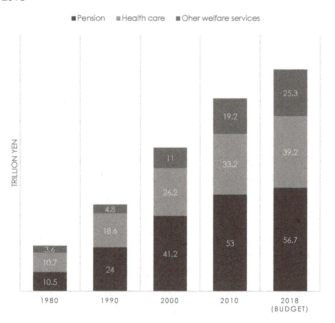

Source: Ministry of Health, Labour and Welfare.

Japan's healthcare provision is among the best in the world both in terms of the high level of technology and the wide availability of specialist doctors (not general practitioners). Japan's spending on healthcare in 2016 as a percentage of GDP was 10.9 per cent, being higher than the UK's (9.8%) but slightly lower than France's (11.5%). The percentage of the US was much higher at 17.1 per cent. However, the US lacks nationwide universal healthcare, despite the enactment of the so-called "Obamacare", and its health insurance system is complex.

Figure 3.12 Government spending on pensions, percentage of GDP, selected countries, 2017

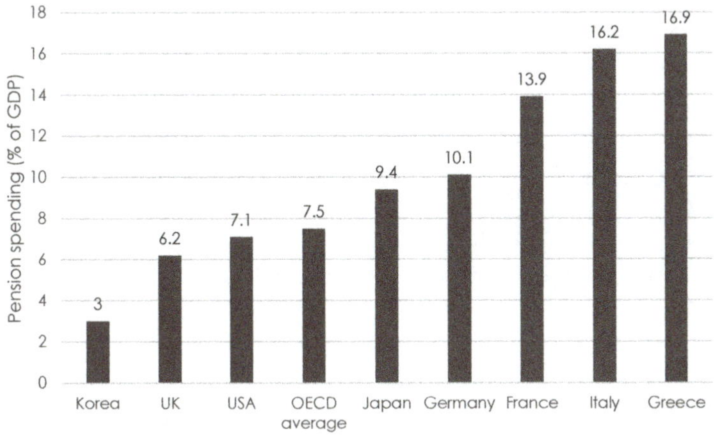

Source: OECD Data 2017 or latest available.

As for government spending on elderly (long-term) care, the percentage of Japan's spending as a percentage of GDP was 2.1 per cent in 2014 and was higher than the OECD average (1.3%), including the US (0.5%) and the UK (1.2%). This is understandable, given the high percentage of elderly people in Japan. Nevertheless, both Sweden (3.2%) and the Netherlands (4.3%) had higher government spending percentages than Japan.

The amount of government spending on unemployment insurance (mostly government payments to the unemployed) has been small in international comparison. Among the OECD countries, Japan's unemployment spending in 2015 was among the lowest, along with the UK, at 0.17 per cent of GDP. The OECD average was 0.68 per cent although countries such as France and Belgium spent 1.62 per cent and 2.95 per cent respectively. Although Japan's unemployment rate has been low in international comparison, it was in an increasing trend throughout the 1970s and the first half of the 1980s before the bubble economy in the late 1980s and again on the rise during the "lost decades" of the 1990s and 2000s until it started to decline in the 2010s (see Figure 3.13). The low amount of spending on unemployment insurance by the Japanese government has been problematic, since the only safety net available to unemployed people once the period of unemployment insurance is completed is social (public) assistance, which is very difficult to qualify for due to its strict conditions of entitlement. This means that only an insufficient amount of unemployment insurance is available to most Japanese workers for a short period (between 90 and 360 days depending on the reason for leaving a job, the length of the period of previous work, etc.).

Figure 3.13 Unemployment rates in Japan, 1955–2015

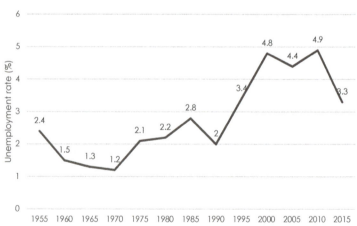

Source: e-Stat Japan.

Although Japan might once have been considered a country of the "middle-class", it is less clearly so when its inequality is measured. Using the Gini coefficient – the typical measure of income or wealth distribution of a nation's citizens – Japan's Gini coefficient in 2017 was 0.34, which was higher than several OECD countries, including Sweden (0.28), France (0.29), Germany (0.29) and Italy (0.33). Only a small number of OECD countries such as the UK and the US had higher Gini coefficients (0.35 and 0.39 respectively). In terms of the relative poverty rate, which is the percentage of people whose annual income is below the poverty line (50% of national median income), Japan's rate in 2017 was 15.7 per cent – higher than those of France (8.3%), Germany (10.4%) and even the UK (11.1%) and Italy (13.7%). The US was the only developed OECD country that had a higher rate (17.8%).

Figure 3.14 Percentage of total population aged 65 and over in Japan, 1980–2015

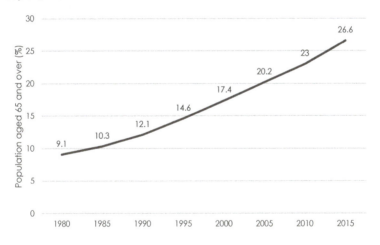

Source: Statistics Bureau, *Statistical Handbook of Japan* (2018).

When wealth distribution is examined by age group, older people in Japan have a larger amount of assets on average, as those in other OECD countries, and a significant age gap can be identified. According to Japan's Statistics Bureau, those aged 29 or younger had ¥3.8 million of savings in 2018 and the amounts increased as people grew older (¥23.3 million among those aged 60–69 although the savings of those aged 70 and over had a slightly lower average of ¥22.5 million). The same trend can be identified in stock investments and home ownership. While those aged 29 or below had only invested ¥200,000 on average in stock, those aged 70 or above invested ¥3.9 million on average. In the case of home ownership, the rate was 30.6 per cent among those aged 29 or below while it was 93.3 per cent among those aged 70 or above.

Japan's aging population has serious implications for the maintenance of the welfare state. The percentage of the population aged 65 and over has been increasing, having grown to 26.6 per cent in 2015 compared to 9.1 per cent in 1980 (see Figure 3.14). In 2015, Japan had the highest percentage of the population aged 65 and above (26.6%) of any country. In 2060, the percentage is projected to increase to 38.1 per cent, followed by countries such as Korea (37.1%) and Italy (33.4%). In 2017, Japanese women had the highest life expectancy (87.3 years) in the world (Japanese men also had one of the highest life expectancies at 81.1 years). This aging population has already strained the government budget but will do so even more in the future and could jeopardize the sustainability of national pension, healthcare insurance and other social welfare services unless drastic cuts to welfare budget are made soon. The increasing number of elderly people is likely to mean meager welfare services in the future, as shown by the recent controversy on the report issued by the Financial Agency stating that individuals would likely need an extra ¥20 million in addition to the national pension to provide for them if they are to live to 100 years old.

4

The structure of the Japanese economy

As outlined in the previous chapters, the Japanese economy experienced high growth in the 1960s and relatively high growth up to the late 1980s in international comparison. However, the Japanese economy has suffered from stagnation and low growth since the collapse of the bubble economy in the early 1990s. Although the structure of Japan's economy has been transformed significantly in some sectors to cope with economic stagnation, we can also identify some continuities in the structure of the economy despite pressure from globalization and regional economic integration in East Asia and the Asia Pacific. While we can see some structural transformations characteristic of American-style capitalism, we can also identify the continuity of structures distinctly Japanese and different from other capitalisms such as America's.

This chapter will examine the main characteristics of Japanese capitalism. It will begin with an analysis of the state–market relations in Japan by examining the concept and practice of the "developmental state" and its transformation and continuity. The chapter will refer to several case studies of industrial policy implemented by the Ministry of International Trade and Industry (MITI, later Ministry of Economy, Trade and Industry, METI), including the recent initiatives aimed at promoting liberalization in certain economic sectors, such as energy, as well as those aimed at protecting national competitiveness as seen in the rescue of high-tech electronics companies that were financially in trouble. The chapter will then examine the role and function of *keiretsu* (corporate groups) as Japanese business networks. It will first examine "vertical" *keiretsu* (large companies and SMEs in the same business group) and identify the important, but often exploited, roles of SMEs in these business networks as well as the advantages for SMEs to be in a vertical *keiretsu*. The chapter will then examine the role and function of "horizontal" *keiretsu* (a business network of large group companies in different industrial sectors) and the institutional complementarities among several economic sectors within a *keiretsu*. The chapter will refer to the so-called "varieties of capitalism" (VoC) literature and criticize the rigid, apolitical VoC perspective of institutional complementarity. The chapter will also discuss the convergence and diversity among capitalisms, including Japanese, under neoliberal globalization in relation to the VoC literature. For this purpose, the deregulation of the Japanese economy in sectors such as finance and labour will be discussed. The chapter will then investigate the "dual" economy in Japan, both competitive and efficient manufacturing sectors (such as the automobile industry and, until recently, electrical appliances and electronics) and non-competitive and inefficient service sectors (such as finance, insurance and retail). The chapter will discuss the causes of efficiency and inefficiency in these different economic sectors from the perspective of state–market relations. In this respect, the chapter will examine the previous "convoy" system in the financial sector and the low degree of internationalization of the economy in terms of inward FDI. Finally, the chapter will consider the impact of regional economic integration in East Asia and the Asia Pacific on Japan's economic policy and competitiveness in the context of the economic rise of China.

THE "DEVELOPMENTAL STATE" AND STATE–MARKET RELATIONS IN JAPAN

Scholars have sought to identify the main characteristics of Japanese capitalism, especially since Japan achieved such high economic growth in the

1960s. One of the classic treatments is Chalmers Johnson's *MITI and the Japanese Miracle*, which was first published in 1982. Johnson classified capitalism into three distinct types: "market rational", "plan ideological" and "plan rational" (Johnson 1982). Capitalisms characterized as "market rational", such as American, are based on the free market principle and have little state intervention in the economy to guide private sector corporations in a direction the government desires. In contrast, communist economies, such as the former Soviet Union's, which maintain government control of the economy almost in every aspect, are categorized as "plan ideological". In "plan rational" economies, such as Japan's, government does not dictate all the economic activities as in the case of "plan ideological" economies. Instead, the government directs and collaborates with the private sector for the purpose of economic growth and development. The "plan rational" government attempts to make rational economic plans in a way to enable private sector corporations to maximize their profits in the domestic market and to compete with foreign companies in the international market. In the Japanese case, it was the Ministry of International Trade and Industry (MITI) that performed the main role in enhancing the competitiveness of Japanese companies and achieving economic development by implementing industrial policy (Johnson 1982).

Japan is a quintessential "developmental state" according to Johnson. For developmental states, such as Japan, economic development is the number one priority. However, economic development is not for the benefit of citizens as consumers but for the sake of the nation state. The origin of the Japanese developmental state could first be identified at the time of imperialism, especially during the war-time economy of the 1930s and first half of the 1940s (Gao 2001; Noguchi 1998). Japan needed to ensure its national survival in a situation where it was forced to conclude unfair treaties with western imperial powers soon after the end of its policy of isolation (*sakoku*) in the 1850s, near the end of the Edo period. "Rich nation, strong army" became the national slogan after the Meiji Restoration in 1868, and the government promoted industrialization in order to be recognized as equal by western powers and to survive the imperial system dominated by them. In this sense, Japan's industrialization after the end of isolation was based on the economic nationalism and neo-mercantilism of the German historical school (the ideas of Friedrich List in particular) and the economic theory of late development of Alexander Gerschenkron (Chang 1999: 182; Cumings 1999: 61; Levi-Faur 1997; Pempel 1999a: 139; Stubbs 2009; Woo-Cumings 1999: 4–10).

However, it was during the 1930s and the first half of the 1940s that the essence of the Japanese developmental state was formed (Gao 2001; Noguchi 1998). To prepare for world war, the military government intervened in the economy extensively with cooperation from the *zaibatsu*. "Reformist" bureaucrats filled with economic nationalism implemented war-time economic plans in the manner of "state socialism" until Japan was defeated in August 1945 (Fukui 1989: 126–37). However, in contrast to the military, the *zaibatsu* and those nationalistic politicians who were purged from their previous powerful positions, many bureaucrats survived the purge and remained in place during the US occupation of Japan. As explained in Chapter 1, the US authority needed bureaucrats' cooperation to implement the occupation policy in an efficient manner. It was MITI bureaucrats, who had escaped from the purge during the US occupation, that performed an essential role in achieving Japan's economic miracle in the 1960s by implementing the industrial policy.

Industrial policy was an essential tool for MITI to achieve economic growth and enhance the competitiveness of Japanese companies in the international market. MITI identified such industries as steel and petrochemicals as strategic sectors for growth and allocated scarce foreign currency reserves to their support during the time of postwar economic reconstruction. This industrial policy is generally considered to have been successful in raising national champions in several industrial sectors and to have been fundamental to Japan's economic reconstruction and later economic growth. MITI led and coordinated with private-sector companies in the implementation of industrial policy to promote investment in the strategic sectors identified by it. MITI provided both incentives and disincentives to induce private-sector companies to take business action in a way it desired rather than forcing them to do so by implementing measures in the form of "administrative guidance", which did not have legal force but which private-sector business still found difficult to ignore or refuse because of the possibility of retaliation or unfavourable treatment by MITI in the case of non-compliance. However, industrial policy was often aimed at achieving mutual benefits for both the government and private-sector companies, rather than the state taking a confrontational stance towards the market (Johnson 1999: 47–50, 56–60).

In contrast, scholars who have emphasized the role of the market (business interest groups as well as economic institutions) in Japan's economic growth and development, have argued that MITI's industrial policy was not always successful at enhancing the competitiveness of the economy (Calder 1993; Friedman 1988; Okimoto 1989; Samuels 1987; Uriu 1996). They cite, for example, as mentioned in Chapter 1, MITI's attempt to rationalize the automobile industry in 1955 by merging several car companies to create a national champion that would produce cheap but high-quality cars, which those companies resisted and the merger did not materialize (Kume 2000: 78–9). Given the competitiveness of the Japanese car industry, MITI's attempt might have been counterproductive.

Scholars have also pointed out that MITI's industrial policy was not only the pro-competitive policy of the developmental state but also an anti-competitive and protective policy. For example, MITI implemented anti-competitive policies to protect domestic industries that were not efficient or productive from international competition (Elder 2003). Such policies included regulations aimed at deterring foreign companies from entering the Japanese market and allowing inefficient industrial sectors to form cartels so that those sectors would be better able to generate profits (Kohno 2003: 99; Tilton & Choi 2007: 19). In addition, this anti-competitive industrial policy also functioned to protect and maintain jobs in inefficient sectors or SMEs (Kume 2000: 72–6, 83; Miwa 1995: 427). In the case of "troubled industries" such as cement and petrochemical, MITI's industrial policy was aimed at protecting the least competitive companies in each industry and supporting the production cartels that enabled those non-competitive companies to survive (Uriu 1996: 253–6). For this reason, Johnson has been criticized for not paying sufficient attention to socio-economic coalitions or interest group politics and instead focused on state bureaucracy and the pro-competitive aspect of the industrial policy of Japan's developmental state (Pempel 1999a: 144–5).

In Japan's interest group politics, which has typically involved inefficient industries such as agriculture, construction, finance and retail, the LDP *zoku* politicians have functioned as intermediaries or the "pipeline" that connects interest groups and the national bureaucratic ministries with the jurisdiction of the relevant sectors. In response to LDP *zoku* politicians' demands, the relevant ministries, including MITI, have implemented anti-competitive, protective policies for the benefit of the relevant interest groups in inefficient and unproductive industries. Seen in these terms, MITI's industrial policy is different from the industrial policy portrayed by Johnson in his *MITI and the Japanese Miracle*. The "iron triangle" of the LDP government, the bureaucracy and big business (*sei, kan, zai*) has been identified as the most powerful interest group in Japan. However, Japan's interest groups include not only big business but also SMEs in inefficient economic sectors (Okumura 1994: 53, 65–8). Aoki Masahiko has claimed that Japan was transformed from the quintessential "developmental" state to a "bureaucratic pluralist" state, where bureaucrats as well as the LDP *zoku* politicians were engaged in distributing economic benefits among several interest groups (for example, the Ministry of Construction and the LDP construction *zoku* politicians who worked for the construction industry) (Aoki 1999: 25). However, the income transfer from industrial sectors with higher productivity, such as automobile industry and electronics, to those sectors with lower productivity, such as construction and agriculture, might have become difficult to maintain due to the increasing competitive pressures on the higher productivity sectors from neighbouring Asian countries. Low productivity sectors in a problematic situation would also demand more protection from the LDP government and bureaucracy.

Whether Japan can best be described as a developmental state or a bureaucratic pluralist state, Japanese society is "corporate-centered" and the consideration of consumer benefits are second to the benefits of corporations. The mentality of *"kan-son min-pi"*, ("respect bureaucrats and despise people") prevailed until the collapse of the bubble economy in the early 1990s, when Japanese people first began to question the credibility of bureaucrats in the light of the economy's poor performance and numerous scandals involving bureaucrats. In Japan's corporate-centered society, pro-consumer competition policy has been weak, partly as a legacy of the developmental state, and instead pro-business policy has been dominant (see Tilton & Choi 2007 in the case of Japan's information and communications industries). Also, it is important to note that in some sectors, Japanese companies have played an important role in providing social welfare benefits such as housing provision instead of the government (Nagano 1994: 262; Osawa 1993). Social welfare provision by corporations has been the Japanese model of privatized social welfare, and Japanese companies have played the dual role of competing in business and maintaining the jobs of their employees (Gao 2001: 47). This has increased the loyalty of regular workers in large companies towards their companies and has been useful for employers to maintain a harmonious relationship with employees. This has also enabled the government to maintain a relatively small government in comparison to some other countries such as Scandinavian.

Although MITI/METI has remained one of the main actors of the Japanese developmental state, its characteristics have not remained unchanged. For example, Kohno argues that MITI/METI has been transformed from a "regulatory" agency into a "deregulatory" agency and promoted deregulation of the economy, although he admits MITI/METI has also been engaged in the protection of SMEs (Kohno 2003: 99–103). It is true, as he argues, that METI has become a deregulatory agency in some tightly-regulated business sectors such as energy (electricity and gas), as seen in the recent liberalization measures introduced by METI (such as the separation of electricity generation and its retail and the liberalization of entry to the energy sector). However, it is also true that METI has demonstrated its continuing developmental state characteristic based on economic nationalism (see Hall 2004 about this point in the case of the liberalization and deregulation of the Japanese economy). For example, METI led the attempt to rescue Elpida Memory, a semi-conductor company producing DRAM (dynamic random-access memory) in 2009. Its aim of injecting tax-payers' money in order to prevent the acquisition of Elpida by a foreign company and the transfer of Japanese technology overseas ultimately failed and Elpida went bankrupt in 2012. It was acquired by Micron Technology, a US semi-conductor company in 2013.

In a similar manner, METI led the rescue measures of Renesas Electronics, a semi-conductor company created through the integration of NEC electronics and Renesas Technology, a joint venture by Hitachi and Mitsubishi Electric. When Renesas Electronics was in trouble financially in 2012 and KKR, a US equity investment company, planned to acquire Renesas Electronics, Japanese carmakers such as Toyota and Nissan opposed the deal. Those Japanese carmakers, which were engaged in business transactions with Renesas Electronics, feared a decrease in their power to negotiate the prices of Renesas products. In response to their request, METI blocked the acquisition by KKR and instead made the Innovation Network Corporation of Japan (INCJ, *Sangyō Kakushin Kikō*), a public-private partnership between the Japanese government and several major Japanese corporations under the supervision of METI, become the largest shareholder of Renesas Electronics. Although the INCJ was founded as a corporation to invest in companies of innovation, it has functioned to some extent as METI's tool to rescue Japanese companies in trouble. METI's objective was again the rescue of "Japanese" industries such as electronics that it sees as vital to Japan's international competitiveness, and the prevention of the transfer of Japanese high technology overseas by preventing foreign acquisition (Nihon Keizai Shimbun 2013a). METI's implementation of industrial policy in these cases was based on economic nationalism of the Japanese developmental state.

METI's attempts to rescue electronics and other manufacturing companies did not end with Renesas, however. More recently there have been the cases of Sharp and Toshiba. In the case of Sharp, METI planned the INCJ's investment in Sharp to rescue the company. METI then attempted to reorganize the Japanese electronics sector by instigating a merger between the liquid crystal display (LCD) sections of Sharp and Japan Display Inc., an electronics company financially in trouble and owned by the INCJ, as well as another merger of the white good sections between Sharp and Toshiba, which was also financially in trouble. However, Sharp was eventually acquired by Taiwan's Hon Hai Precision Industry (Foxconn), a gigantic company of original equipment manufacturing, and METI's reorganization plan failed (Nihon Keizai Shimbun 2016).

The case of Toshiba was similar. Toshiba had suffered from a huge loss due to the bankruptcy of its US subsidiary Westinghouse, which was engaged in the business of nuclear power plants. To make up for this loss, Toshiba planned to sell Toshiba Memory, its most profitable subsidiary. However, METI, afraid of the transfer of Toshiba Memory's high technology to foreign companies, especially Chinese, intervened in the sale. Eventually, METI was successful in facilitating the purchase of a majority of the shares by Japanese companies, including Toshiba, and the rest by US and South Korean companies including Bain Capital, SK Hynix, Apple and Dell (Nihon Keizai Shimbun 2017). However, it is doubtful whether this acquisition was made from an economically rational perspective.

More recently, the export projects of nuclear power plants led by METI have ended in failure. The current Abe administration has aimed to export nuclear power plants overseas to maintain Japan's nuclear power plant industry and its knowhow in Japan after the triple disasters of March 2011. However, with Hitachi's abandonment of the nuclear power plant project in the UK, all these projects had failed by early 2019 (Asahi Shimbun 2019a; Nihon Keizai Shimbun 2019b). These projects led by METI have demonstrated its quintessential industrial policy based on economic nationalism of the Japanese developmental state, but all of them have ended in failure.

KEIRETSU AND INSTITUTIONAL COMPLEMENTARITIES
IN THE JAPANESE ECONOMY

A *Keiretsu* – for example Mitsui or Mitsubishi – is a group of companies with interlocking business relationships. *Keiretsu* were the *zaibatsu* (economic conglomerates) before the Second World War that controlled the Japanese economy by monopolizing many sectors such as banking, heavy chemical industry, retail and real estate. The *zaibatsu* were dissolved by the US occupation authority after the war as they were considered to have cooperated with the military to pursue the war. However, with the advent of the Cold War, US occupation policy changed from the demilitarization and democratization of Japan, which also aimed at keeping its economy weak, to the remilitarization and strengthening of the economy as Japan became an important capitalist ally and the location for US military bases (the so-called "reverse course"). As a result, the former *zaibatsu* business-people who were first purged by the US occupation authority were able to return to important positions in the Japanese economy during the reverse in US policy. At the same time, the implementation of the Anti-Monopoly Law was relaxed and again after Japan regained independence with the signing of the San Francisco Peace Treaty in 1952 and the creation of the business-friendly LDP government in 1955. However, the name "*zaibatsu*" had a tainted connotation as a military collaborator, so the name "*keiretsu*" became more commonly used. In addition, there were differences between the older *zaibatsu* conglomerates and the *keiretsu*. One of the most significant was, while the business families such as Mitsui, Mitsubishi and Sumitomo that owned holding companies controlled the companies in their *zaibatsu*, holding companies were banned in the *keiretsu* as a result of the implementation of the Anti-Monopoly Law by the US occupation force after the Second World War.

In the postwar Japanese economy, we can identify both "vertical" and "horizontal" *keiretsu*. Vertical *keiretsu* are a group formed of a leading large company with SMEs under its control, most typically seen in the manufacturing sectors. Those SMEs either supply parts that cooperate upstream with the leading company or they distribute the products made by the leading company and so cooperate downstream (Hatch 2010: 54–6; Hatch & Yamamura 1996: 70–72). For example, Toyota Motor Corporation has many SMEs under its control that are specialized in the production of car components such as chassis, lights, windshields, brakes, airbags, tyres, semi-conductors such as micro-controllers and so on. Some of these SMEs are subsidiaries of the leading companies, but even where there is no shareholding relationship, the leading companies can exercise strong control over the production activities of other affiliated companies in the same vertical *keiretsu*. When the business of the leading companies is not going well, for example, or when they need to increase price competitiveness, these subsidiaries and other SMEs in the same vertical *keiretsu* can be pressured to reduce the prices of their products used by the leading companies, as was the case in Renesas Electronics and the car companies Toyota and Nissan already mentioned (Nihon Keizai Shimbun 2013a). While the leading companies can transfer price risk to their subsidiaries or affiliated companies and maintain price competitiveness in this way, their subsidiaries and other affiliated SMEs are often put into difficulties as a result of the leading companies' exploitation of their weaker position. The leading companies can also focus on core activities and maintain human resource management strategies, such as lifetime employment, by using subsidiaries and affiliated companies to save on labour costs (Westney 1999: 168–9).

However, there are some advantages to being in a vertical *keiretsu* for subsidiaries and affiliated SMEs. For example, their leading company can act as guarantor for securing bank loans. And the transfer of employees from the leading company to subsidiaries or affiliated companies, whether on a temporary or permanent basis, could also be useful for maintaining communication with the leading company and for acquiring technologies and business know-how from the leading company, although this technological transfer could also work in the opposite direction (Westney 1999: 164–5). The transfer of employees among companies within a vertical *keiretsu* and the prevalence of firm-specific or *keiretsu*-specific skills may explain why interfirm labour mobility has been low between Japanese companies that belong to different *keiretsu*. Vertical *keiretsu* have also functioned as a non-tariff barrier for the entry into the Japanese market by foreign companies due to the existence of long-term business relationships between leading companies and their subsidiaries and affiliates (Westney 1999: 169–70).

In contrast, "horizontal" *keiretsu* are business groups made up of large companies in *different* economic sectors. For example, the horizontal *keiretsu* of Mitsubishi includes the former Mitsubishi Bank (currently Mitsubishi-UFJ Bank), Mitsubishi Corporation (trading company, "*shōsha*"), Mitsubishi Heavy Industry, Mitsubishi Automobile, Mitsubishi Real Estate, Mitsubishi Chemical, and so on. Before Japanese banks suffered from the problem of non-performing loans, a horizontal *keiretsu* included a "main bank" (in the case of the Mitsubishi *keiretsu*, the former Mitsubishi Bank). The origin of the main bank goes back to the war-time economy when the military government needed to ensure the financing of the munitions industry by indirect financing of bank loans rather than by direct financing of stock issue to reduce investment risks (Gao 2001: 59–61). The main bank monitored business activities and performance of the companies in the same *keiretsu* by sending its employees as directors to those companies. In return, the main bank provided long-term loans with low interest rates to those companies in the same *keiretsu*. As a result, companies in a *keiretsu* were able to put the expansion of market share ahead of long-term business profits. This was also facilitated due to "cross shareholding" among *keiretsu* companies, i.e. *keiretsu* companies owning shares in other companies in the same *keiretsu* (Okumura 1994: 57–60). With cross shareholding, companies were able to avoid the strong pressure from individual and organizational shareholders who sought short-term profits, as the majority of shareholders of each *keiretsu* company were companies in the same *keiretsu*. Cross-shareholding also deterred inward FDI in Japanese companies by foreign companies through merger and acquisition, as did the closed business relationships based on vertical *keiretsu* (Blomström *et al.*, 2001: 258; Okumura 1994: 61–4).

Hall and Soskice have argued that the good performance of the economy depends on the complementarity, or good fit, of its economic institutions, and in the case of the Japanese economy, several scholars have identified institutional complementarities among the companies in the horizontal *keiretsu* (Aoki 1999: 16–19; Gao 2001, for example). The provision of cheap long-term loans by the main bank to group companies which facilitated a long-term business perspective rather than the pressure to achieve quick profits, and the cross-shareholding among *keiretsu* companies that protected them from foreign company involvement and investment companies seeking profits from capital gains, are all examples of institutional complementarity. Furthermore, as a result of the long-term orientation of *keiretsu* companies, they were able to provide lifetime employment to their workers, and in return those employees showed their commitment by working for many hours, often without fully receiving overtime pay. This contributed to amicable industrial relations and the strong performance of Japanese companies. Enterprise unions, which mostly represented the interests of regular workers in large companies, cooperated with employers to maintain the competitiveness and profitability of their companies, and employers protected their jobs in return.

However, the importance of institutional complementarities for the functioning of the economy depends on the economic conditions under which each institution can function properly. It is possible to argue that the favourable domestic and international economic situations were necessary conditions for proper functioning of those economic institutions and the institutional complementarities among different economic sectors before the collapse of the bubble economy in the early 1990s. Since then, the failure of one or two institutions to perform properly has led to the malfunction of other institutions and ultimately the whole system. For example, as a result of the collapse of the bubble economy and the emergence of non-performing loans, it became difficult for the largest bank in each *keiretsu* to continue to function as the main bank and to provide cheap, long-term loans, which in turn has made it more difficult for companies in the same *keiretsu* to maintain a long-term perspective for their business and continue to offer lifetime employment. The erosion of lifetime employment has prompted some employees to leave their company, affecting companies' ability to maintain the high skills necessary to compete in a more globalized economy. The change in corporate governance resulting from the failure of the main bank system and the decrease in cross shareholding as a result of the weakened financial capacity of Japanese companies to maintain stocks of other *keiretsu* companies also increased the importance of shareholders outside the *keiretsu*, which led to an increased demand for short-term profits by those shareholders. Institutional complementarities may have functioned well in the Japanese economy but only at a time of high economic growth and in an international economic context with low pressure from globalization.

CONVERGENCE AND DIVERSITY AMONG CAPITALISMS UNDER NEOLIBERAL GLOBALIZATION

In the "varieties of capitalism" (VoC) literature, Japan along with Germany are categorized as coordinated market economies (CMEs) (Hall & Soskice 2001). Whereas, countries such as the United States and the UK are categorized as liberal market economies (LMEs). In CMEs, the complementarities among economic institutions, such as financial provision, corporate governance, industrial relations, skills training and so on, can be seen to enhance the function of other economic institutions in a complementary manner, as seen above in the Japanese case. However, these institutional complementarities based on coordination that are characteristic of CMEs are absent from LMEs. VoC scholars such as Hall and Soskice have claimed that LMEs and CMEs will not converge even with strong pressure from globalization and neither will CMEs become more like LMEs despite the strong market discipline exerted by globalization. Instead, they argue, CMEs will seek to strengthen coordination among economic institutions even further so that the companies would be better able to survive in a more competitive business environment under

globalization. In contrast to LMEs, where we would expect further deregulation of the economy, CMEs would attempt to increase their economic
efficiency and competitiveness through further coordination (Hall & Soskice 2001; Hall & Thelen 2009; Kitschelt *et al.* 1999). In this way, LMEs
and CMEs will not converge even under the strongest pressure from neoliberalism and globalization and will maintain diversity based on their
own institutional complementarities.

Although the influence of neoliberalism may have declined some-
what recently from the spread of economic inequality and the rise of
right-wing populism, it remains a powerful economic ideology. And there
are scholars, in contrast to the VoC adherents, who emphasize the dominant influence of neoliberalism and the increasing degree of liberalization
of world economies, whether LMEs or CMEs (Baccaro & Howell 2011;
Cerny *et al.* 2005; Howell & Givan 2011; Kalinowski 2015; Streeck 2009).
Indeed, some scholars, (for example, Cerny *et al.*) have not only emphasized the strong converging force of globalization and the neoliberal
transformation of world economies but have also stressed differences in
the neoliberal transformation of capitalisms, due to differences in domestic political and economic institutions. Thus, these scholars argue that we
see the emergence of "varieties of neoliberalism", not the continuation of
"varieties of capitalism" (Cerny *et al.* 2005).

In the Japanese case, we can identify some market-oriented changes
in financial and labour markets such as Big Bang financial deregulation
in the 1990s and the deregulation of the labour market since the late
1990s (Watanabe 2012, 2014, 2015a, 2015c). These changes in the Japanese economy are characteristic of LMEs. However, we can also identify
business practices that do not conform to market disciplines in several
economic sectors, especially those inefficient sectors such as agriculture,
construction, retail and finance supported by the LDP government. In this
respect, the VoC interpretive framework can be criticized for its exclu-
sive focus on "competitive" sectors of the economy with supposedly tight
institutional complementarities. However, as seen above, the state's "compensation" role can be widely seen in the inefficient sectors of the Japanese

economy. So while it may be the case that some business practices in some sectors of the economy may have converged to those of LMEs, there are several others that do not conform to the business practices based on market disciplines associated with (some sectors of) LMEs. In any case, the VoC scholars' claim that CMEs would strengthen coordination, rather than implement deregulation, under intensified neoliberal globalization is more difficult to support at times of economic hardship due to the growing urgency for employers to reduce labour costs and increase flexibility and so diminish their capacity to maintain, much less strengthen, coordination.

JAPAN'S "DUAL" ECONOMY

Japan can be said to have a "dual" economy in two respects. Firstly, there are differences between large companies and SMEs in terms of profitability, labour productivity, employees' wages and so on. Secondly, there are "efficient" and "inefficient" sectors within the Japanese economy (efficient sectors such as manufacturing, especially cars, and inefficient sectors such as finance, retail and construction) and the differences between these sectors are stark. There are also "dual" labour markets composed of regular and non-regular employment, but this will be discussed in the next chapter.

In Japan, 99.7 per cent of companies are SMEs and only 0.3 per cent are "large" companies.[9] However, in terms of the number of employees (14.3 million employees in large companies and 33.6 million employees in SMEs), the disparity is less marked. Large companies have higher productivity on average compared to SMEs. The recurring profits of large companies were around 50 per cent larger than those of SMEs in 2008 (¥15.6 trillion compared to ¥10.3 trillion). However, the gap has widened since then. In 2017, the recurring profits of large companies were ¥57.6 trillion while those of SMEs were ¥21.3 trillion (see Figure 4.1).

In terms of wages, there is also a disparity between large companies and SMEs with higher monthly median wages in large companies.

Although the wage gap between large companies and SMEs for workers aged 20–24 was around ¥50,000 a month in 2015, the gap widened as the age bracket went up with the largest disparity in the age group 50–54 of ¥144,000: ¥461,000 compared to ¥317,000 (see Figure 4.2). The median monthly wages of regular workers in large companies were around 50 per cent higher than those of regular workers in SMEs in this age bracket.

Figure 4.1 Recurring profits of large Japanese companies and SMEs, 2008–17

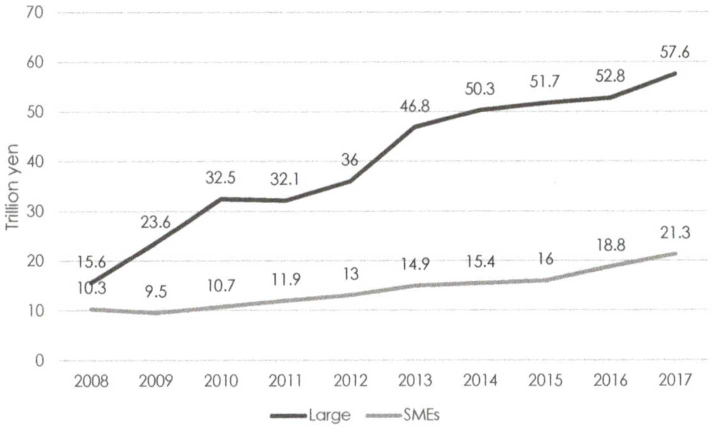

Source: Ministry of Finance, *Corporate Statistics*.

As for the dualism in efficiency (in terms of profitability, productivity and so on), Japan's efficient economic sectors are mostly in manufacturing, with the automobile sector among the most efficient and competitive. Companies such as Toyota, Nissan and Honda are internationally competitive, having invested a huge amount of capital in overseas markets. Electronics companies such as Sony, Matsushita (Panasonic), Toshiba, NEC and Fujitsu are no longer so competitive internationally, particularly in some products such as semi-conductors, televisions and personal computers. Sanyo, which used to produce a range of electronic products, went bankrupt and was acquired by Panasonic. Similarly, Sharp, once also competitive and producing many popular electronics products, saw their business operation run into difficulties and was eventually acquired by Hong Hai (Foxconn), a gigantic Taiwanese company specializing in electronics manufacturing services. Toshiba, famous once for its laptop computer "Dynabook", recently accumulated sizeable levels of debt due to the bankruptcy of its subsidiary Westinghouse, a US company that built nuclear power plants. Toshiba managed to survive only by receiving capital injection from a coalition of Japanese, US and South Korean companies and selling Toshiba Memory, its top-performing subsidiary that specialized in the production of memory sticks.

Figure 4.2 Monthly wages of regular employees by age (large companies vs SMEs), 2015

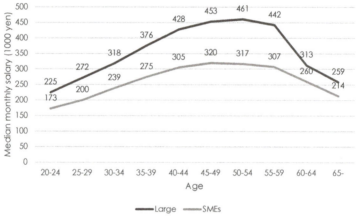

Source: MHLW, *Wage Structure Basic Survey*, 2017.

In contrast to (previously) efficient and competitive economic sectors mentioned above, Japan has several inefficient economic sectors, mostly in services such as finance and retail but also in construction and agriculture. There are several reasons why these economic sectors are inefficient, but chief among them is government protection. For example, the Ministry of Finance (MOF) implemented the so-called "convoy system" to protect inefficient banks and maintain financial stability. When banks, especially small and medium-sized ones, were near bankruptcy, relatively stronger, larger banks were encouraged to acquire them in order to maintain stability in the financial sector. However, the convoy system also created moral hazard and inefficiencies. In addition, many government regulations restrained competition among banks, such as regulations to limit the number and location of bank branches and ATMs, business hours, the spread between lending and borrowing interest rates and so on. As will be discussed in detail in Chapter 6, the Japanese banking sector is inefficient and operates outside of international industry standards in many respects. For example, for many years the business hours of Japanese bank branches were 9am to 3pm, and it is only now that these are changing. Also, except for ATMs in 7-Eleven convenience stores and a few others, most Japanese bank ATMs do not accept bank cards issued by non-Japanese banks.

Figure 4.3 Inward FDI, selected countries, percentage of GDP, 2013–16

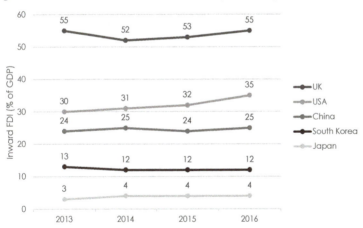

Source: OECD, *Foreign Direct Investment Statistics*, 2019.

The very low level of inward FDI in Japan (less than 5% of GDP) is also a reason for the existence of inefficient economic sectors (see Figure 4.3 comparing inward FDI in Japan and selected countries). The lack of inward FDI, especially the merger and acquisition of Japanese companies by foreign companies, has meant that relatively little new technology and business know-how has been transferred to Japan (Mason 1999: 367). As will be discussed in Chapter 6 in detail, this has contributed to the so-called "Galapagos" syndrome where inefficient sectors of the Japanese economy do not meet global standards, suffers from low productivity and have been little affected by international market mechanisms.

Finally, it is worth mentioning Japan's train services in the context of the dual economy. Although Japanese train services are widely considered to be efficient both inside and outside of Japan, it is only part of the story. It is true that metro and suburban train services in large cities are usually punctual, if not always so, as exaggerated by the foreign mass media. The famous *Shinkansen* bullet trains are certainly fast, if not the fastest in the world, but they are very expensive except for foreign tourists who can use the rail pass issued by Japan Rail. The bullet trains have performed an important role in showcasing Japan's fast and efficient train services for the outside world and are indeed a symbol of Japan's high-tech train system, but they are only part of Japan's railway system and are a good example of Japan's dual economy. Except for the bullet trains, most other trains are very slow and still quite expensive, especially Japan Rail trains in mid- and long-distance services. Most Japanese trains run at speeds of less than 100km per hour (more often less than 50km per hour). However, this is little known or recognized outside Japan, or indeed even within Japan. Instead, the image of the bullet trains as a symbol of Japan's fast and efficient train services has been promoted by the Japanese government and business stemming from national pride and economic nationalism. The Japanese media has also lacked the critical and international perspective necessary to report these slow but expensive train services in Japan to the outside world, although that may be partly due to its lack of news worthiness.

REGIONAL ECONOMIC INTEGRATION
AND THE JAPANESE ECONOMY

During the 1980s the Japanese economy, or more precisely Japanese manufacturing sectors, became internationalized to a greater extent, increasing their investment overseas, especially in East Asia, due to the appreciation of Japanese yen after the Plaza Accord in 1985 and the slight decrease in the competitiveness of their exports in terms of price (Hatch & Yamamura 1996; Nakagawa 2006: 324). In the early 1990s, it was not only large manufacturing companies but also their subcontractors and affiliated companies –the SMEs – that advanced into East Asian markets (Hatch 2010). And in this way, large Japanese manufacturing companies created supply chains composed of their Japanese subsidiaries and affiliated companies in East Asia, often with help from the major trading company (*shōsha*) in the same *keiretsu*. It was as if those large Japanese manufacturing companies exported their domestic *keiretsu* to East Asia. Indeed, Japanese investment often involved using the Japanese SMEs of their subsidiaries instead of local companies. Although the economies in East Asia became more integrated throughout the 1980s and 1990s before the Asian financial crisis, the process was dominated by Japanese companies, which reminds us of the Great East Asia Co-prosperity Zone created by imperialist Japan during the Second World War.

However, the East Asian economies were also undergoing their own structural changes at the same time. In the 1980s, South Korea, Taiwan, Hong Kong and Singapore saw rapid industrialization (Hatch & Yamamura 1996: 27–36) to become competitive "newly industrializing economies" (NIEs). During the 1990s, their economies grew even more competitive and Japan experienced greater competition from them. However, the most significant economic phenomenon in East Asia in recent times has been the rise of China. Since the adoption of the Open-Door Policy by Deng Xiaoping in the late 1970s, China's economy grew even more rapidly than the former NIEs. China received a large amount of foreign direct investment from Japan and other East Asian countries such as Hong Kong. With this process, Japan began to experience so-called "industrial hollowing-out" (*sangyō kūdōka*) – the relocation of manufacturing facilities from Japan to other East Asian countries with lower labour costs, especially mainland China but later also Vietnam, Myanmar and so on (Cowling & Thomlinson 2011). Although some East Asian economies, such as South Korea and Thailand, experienced serious economic setbacks as a result of the Asian financial crisis in the late 1990s, they did regain economic growth after the crisis, whereas Japan suffered from its own financial crisis soon after and its economy remained stagnant.

The Asian financial crisis was a turning point in the balance of economic power between Japan and China in East Asia. In contrast to Japan, which suffered from the Asian financial crisis indirectly and whose proposal of the Asian Monetary Fund was soundly rejected by the US and the IMF, China improved its reputation as a reliable economic power by avoiding both the devaluation of its currency Renminbi and competition with the cheaper export products of those countries negatively affected by the Asian financial crisis (Naughton 1999: 209–10; Pempel 1999b: 228–32). The Chinese economy continued to grow rapidly after the Asian financial crisis and by 2010, had surpassed Japan in terms of economic size measured by the GDP and became the second largest economy in the world after the United States. With the enhanced competitiveness of the former NIEs and the economic rise of China, the East Asian economies have been further integrated, but in a very different way from the previously Japan-dominated process before the Asian financial crisis.

As for the political aspect of regional economic integration, several international economic organizations were established to promote the integration of East Asian and Asia Pacific economies. The Asia Pacific Economic Cooperation (APEC), which was founded in 1989 against the background of regional economic integration in Europe (the Single European Act in 1987) and North America (the US–Canada Free Trade Agreement in 1988), was the forerunner in the regional economic integration process in the Asia Pacific (Beeson 2009: 40–43; Nakagawa 2006: 324–6). However, APEC was ineffective in coping with the Asian financial crisis in the late 1990s and its importance was diminished. Instead, the framework based on either ASEAN Plus Three (the 10 ASEAN countries plus China, Japan and South Korea) or ASEAN Plus Six (the addition of Australia, New Zealand and India) became more important to promote regional economic integration (Beeson 2009: 77–82).

In the 2000s, Japan concluded bilateral free trade agreements (FTAs) with countries in Asia Pacific including the Japan–Singapore FTA in 2002 and the Japan–Mexico FTA in 2005 along with bilateral economic partnership agreements (EPAs) such as the Japan–Philippines EPA in 2006 and the Japan–Indonesia EPA in 2007. Business industries represented by Keidanren (Japan Business Federation) lobbied the LDP government to promote bilateral FTAs and EPAs, hoping that Japanese companies would be able to take advantage of the expansion of business opportunities that FTAs and EPAs brought against a background of stagnant liberalization through the WTO's multilateral channel. Keidanren also hoped FTAs and EPAs would promote the structural reform of the domestic economy intended by the Koizumi administration due to an increase in cheaper imports and the enhanced competition from foreign producers (Nakagawa 2006: 326–9, 331–3).

In 2013, the Abe administration decided to join the negotiation of the US-led Trans-Pacific Partnership (TPP). The TPP was different from previous FTAs in terms of its scope and degree of liberalization. It not only aimed to set a higher degree of trade liberalization in terms of tariff reduction but also aimed to liberalize other economic activities such as FDI and the trade in services. The biggest problem Japan faced in participating in the TPP was the resistance to trade liberalization by its politically powerful agricultural interest groups. Most of Japanese agriculture lacked international competitiveness and depended on the political support of the LDP government, with LDP agricultural *zoku* politicians acting as pipelines between farmers and the Ministry of Agriculture, Forestry and Fisheries (MAFF) and providing agricultural interest groups with subsidies and protective regulations in return for votes and political donations. However, the Abe administration, which enhanced the policy-making power of the Cabinet of the Prime Minister, was able to contain the resistance from agricultural interest groups not only by promising the maintenance of high tariffs for the five most important agricultural products (such as rice) but also by reducing the political power of the JA-Zenchū (Japanese Central Union of Agricultural Cooperatives) as mentioned in Chapter 2 (Ito 2015; Kujiraoka 2016: 102–11; Nishikawa 2017).

Although the twelve countries negotiating TPP eventually reached an agreement in 2016, it was never ratified after the US withdrew its signature. Even after the US withdrawal, Japan strived to reach a new agreement with the remaining countries, despite initial hesitation, and was able to conclude a revised agreement, the Comprehensive and Progressive Trans-Pacific Partnership (CPTPP) in 2018. Japan is also a negotiating member of the Regional Comprehensive Economic Partnership (RCEP) of ASEAN Plus Six. However, the difference in opinion exists between those countries seeking a high degree of liberalization (such as Australia and Japan) and those that are less ambitious due to their large state-owned enterprises (such as China and India). When most member countries were ready to sign the RCEP in November 2019, India withdrew from the RCEP because of its concern that a huge increase in imports from China would be detrimental to its domestic economy (Nihon Keizai Shimbun 2019c). At the time of writing the remaining countries, including Japan, have not reached an agreement. The RCEP without India would make it more difficult for Japan to contain a powerful China, and it appears that Japan is now hesitant to reach an agreement.

5

The human and labour factors of the Japanese economy

This chapter will examine the Japanese economy in terms of the labour market, human resource management, labour market and social policy and labour migration. It will begin with Japan's quintessential characteristics of human resource management: "lifetime employment" and "seniority pay and promotion". The chapter will also examine the problems related to regular employment (but also non-regular employment) such as long working hours and the phenomenon of *karōshi* (death due to overwork) as well as the *hataraki-kata kaikaku* ("Work-Style Reform") recently introduced by the LDP government. This will be followed by an analysis of labour market deregulation since the late 1990s and the increased use of non-regular workers. In relation to the changes and continuities of human resource management, the chapter will discuss cooperative industrial relations based on enterprise unionism. It will then discuss problems in the Japanese labour market such as gender discrimination and inequality, dualism (inequality between regular and non-regular workers in terms of wages, benefits, training, etc.) and poor working conditions.

This chapter will also conduct an analysis of the government policy aimed at improving Japan's low fertility rate, including labour and social policies related to childcare provision and maternity leave from the 1990s and those policies aimed at achieving a better work–life balance proposed by the current Abe administration. The chapter will then discuss the issue of declining population, especially in rural areas, and examine domestic and international labour migration as a possible solution to this problem as well as government immigration policy, including recent changes that opened official routes for the migration of low-skilled workers.

JAPANESE HUMAN RESOURCE MANAGEMENT AND INDUSTRIAL RELATIONS

Japanese human resource management has been characterized by "lifetime employment" and "seniority pay and promotion", especially since the economic miracle in the 1960s. A high percentage of regular workers in large companies (if not SMEs) tend to work for the same company throughout their career until they retire and their pay and promotion prospects depend on their seniority, i.e. how many years they have worked for the company. "Cooperative" labour-management relations has also been identified as a distinctive characteristic of the Japanese labour market: Japanese labour unions, which are mostly composed of "enterprise" unions, have cooperated with employers since the establishment of the "labour-management consensus" based on the institutionalization of lifetime employment and seniority-based pay and promotion in the 1960s (Hasegawa 1993; Nishinarita 1998; Nomura 1994). This cooperation became even more evident after the private-sector unions led by the International Metal Federation-Japan Council (IMF-JC), the industrial federation in Japan's competitive (or previously competitive) sectors such as automobile and electronics, achieved a hegemonic position in the labour movement in the mid-1970s (Kume 1998, 2005).

The origin of lifetime employment in Japan dates back to the 1920s. Japan's heavy manufacturing and chemical industry started to develop then, and companies needed to secure workers with high skills. In order to maintain those highly skilled workers and prevent them from moving to other companies, employers needed to provide an incentive for those workers to stay in their companies (Moriguchi 2014; Moriguchi

& Ono 2006: 156). Lifetime employment as well as seniority-based pay and promotion provided a strong incentive for those workers to remain in the same company for a long time. In the 1960s when Japan achieved its economic miracle, lifetime employment and seniority-based pay and promotion became institutionalized as a result of a consensus between management, mostly represented by Nikkeiren (Japan Federation of Employers' Association) and Keidanren (Japan Federation of Economic Organizations) and labour, represented by cooperative enterprise unions led by Sōhyō (General Council of Trade Unions of Japan) and Dōmei (Japan Confederation of Labor) among others (Hasegawa 1993: 25–6). In the 1970s, when industrialized countries suffered from the oil crises and low economic growth, Japan achieved a relatively high level of economic growth based on this labour–management consensus. Unlike labour unions in other industrialized countries, Japanese unions in the private sector cooperated with management by refraining from conducting strikes and from demanding significant wage rise, which helped Japanese companies survive in a relatively low growth period. In return, management made efforts to maintain lifetime employment, sometimes by transferring employees from the headquarters to subsidiaries in the same *keiretsu*. However, performance-based pay and promotion began to gradually replace seniority-based pay and promotion in the 1970s. The 1980s was mostly a period of economic growth for Japan, especially during the bubble economy in the late 1980s, so the labour–management consensus based on job protection and labour cooperation was mostly maintained.

However, significant changes in human resource management can be identified since the collapse of the bubble economy in the early 1990s in a need for increased flexibility (Debroux 2006; Imai 2011; Watanabe 2012, 2014, 2015a, 2018a). To cope with low economic growth and intensified international and regional economic competition from countries such as South Korea and Taiwan, and then China, Japanese companies, especially those in its most competitive sectors such as automobile and electronics, sought more flexible and lower-cost human resource management. For example, Japanese companies narrowed the scope of lifetime employment by reducing, or in some cases even suspending, the hiring of young university graduates and dismissing or encouraging the voluntary retirement of older regular workers (Ogura 2013: 38–47; see Figure 5.1 for the number of regular and non-regular workers among young workers aged 15–24). The scope for regular workers to receive seniority-based pay also became more limited (Nishinarita 1998: 214). As a result, the salary of regular workers has been stagnant, especially since the 2000s, with the gap between regular and non-regular workers' wages remaining constant (see Figures 5.2 and 5.3). Although seniority-based pay and promotion still exist, the percentage of performance-based pay and promotion has been increasing, especially for those in management positions (Aoki *et al.* 2014; Debroux 2006: 130–31; Imai 2011; Hamaaki *et al.* 2012).

Figure 5.1 Regular and non-regular workers in Japan aged 15–24, 1995–2015

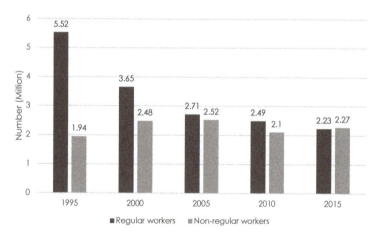

Source: Statistics Bureau, *Labour Force Survey*, 2016.

One of the unique and distinctive aspects of Japanese companies' management of human resources is their recruitment of new university graduates, a process called "*shūshoku ikkatsu saiyō*" in Japanese (literally "simultaneous recruitment of new graduates"). Keidanren (Japan Business

Figure 5.2   Monthly wages of regular workers in Japan, 1990–2015

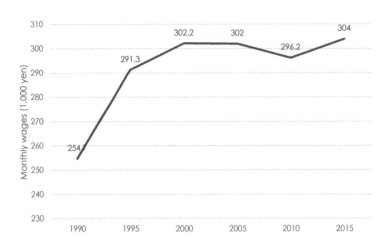

Source: Ministry of Health, Labour and Welfare, *Wage Structure Basic Survey*, 2018.

Figure 5.3   Wage gap between regular and non-regular workers in Japan, 2011–15

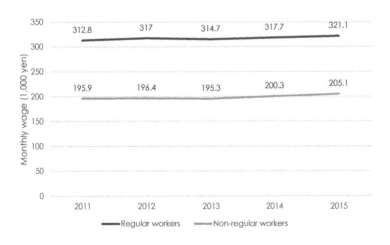

Source: Ministry of Health, Labour and Welfare, *Wage Structure Basic Survey*, 2016.

Federation since its merger with Nikkeiren in 2002) has stipulated the rule for recruiting university graduates and a large majority of Japanese companies have followed this rule (albeit with a certain level of "cheating"). Based on this rule, companies begin their recruitment process (job fairs and rounds of interviews) at the same time (usually before the final year of studies), begin issuing job offers at the same time, and all new university graduates begin their company life on the same day of the year (April 1). This practice, closely related to lifetime employment, has existed for many years. However, significant changes in the domestic and international business environments such as the economic stagnation that followed the collapse of the bubble economy in the early 1990s and intensified global and regional economic competition prompted some corporations to question the usefulness of this practice. Most recently, the new chairman of Keidanren, who is also the current chairman of Hitachi Corporation, announced that Keidanren would not stick to this rule from 2021. However, some companies, especially SMEs, which fear the possibility of more intensified competition in the recruitment of university graduates together with many universities, have expressed concerns about the abolishment of the rule. In response, the current Abe administration has proposed to make a new rule for the period after 2021 (Asahi Shimbun 2018m). From the perspective of some companies in competitive sectors, a more flexible recruitment process that would enable the greater use of skilled middle-aged workers is more useful. For those companies, the raison d'être for simultaneous recruitment of new university graduates has vanished.

As for employment protection, the LDP government attempted to relax existing dismissal rules several times in response to employers' demands. Most recently, the current Abe administration attempted to do so by introducing fiduciary compensation in the case of unfair dismissal instead of reinstatement (the first Abe administration between 2006 and 2007 also made a similar attempt). This attempt was unsuccessful, however, as the Abe administration feared voter backlash at the time of election. Unlike in the case of non-regular workers, a majority of workers in Japan are regular workers, and the introduction of a reform that might threaten their job security could be risky for a governing party. For now, there is no plan to introduce fiduciary compensation in the case of unfair dismissal. Instead, Japanese employers and the current Abe administration have promoted the diversification of regular employment by increasing the number of "semi-regular" workers, as will be discussed later.

In addition, Japanese employers and the LDP government have attempted to increase the flexibility in the use of regular workers by introducing and expanding the scope of "discretionary work". Under discretionary work, working-time rules are relaxed and those regular employees who work under discretionary work do not receive overtime pay except for work over weekends, during holidays and late at night (Imai 2011; Watanabe 2012, 2014). Those workers are assumed to have a certain level of autonomy and discretion in conducting their work and so the link between working hours and pay is reduced. Discretionary work adopts performance-based pay, and annual income is predetermined based on the tasks to be carried out by the relevant worker. Workers may benefit, therefore, from shorter work time by efficiently engaging in their tasks, at least theoretically. In practice, however, workers under discretionary work often must engage in overtime work because of a great amount of workload, for which they are not paid most of the time. In many cases, discretionary work has been used by employers as a measure to cut labour costs by not paying for overtime work.

Discretionary work was introduced by the 1987 amendment to the Labour Standards Law and a category of "professional-type" discretionary work was created for professional workers such as lawyers and certified public accountants. The 1998 amendment to the Labour Standards Law expanded the scope of discretionary work by adding the new category of "planning-type" discretionary work for those "non-professional" white-collar workers who work in administrative positions such as business planning sections in company head offices. The 2003 amendment to the Labour Standards Law further expanded the scope of discretionary work by including white-collar workers in business planning sections even when they do not work in head offices (Watanabe 2012, 2014). Most recently, the current Abe administration has introduced the "highly professional work" category with the Work-Style Reform in 2018. Unlike discretionary workers, regular employees in the category of highly professional work (professional workers such as business consultants and foreign exchange dealers, with an annual income of more than ¥10,750,000, which is around $98,000 at current exchange rates) do not receive overtime pay even when they work during weekends, holidays or late at night. As such, highly professional work is a complete exception to the working-time rules on overtime pay. Although employers can use this categorization only for professional workers with a relatively high annual income, this is nevertheless a deregulatory measure aimed at further increasing the flexibility in the use of regular workers in terms of working-time regulation by completely abolishing overtime pay (Watanabe 2018a).

Before the enactment of the Work-Style Reform in 2018, it was possible for employers to set "unlimited" overtime working hours according to Article 36 of the Labour Standards Law if employers and union representatives had reached such an agreement. Given the balance of power between employers and unions, it was common for employers to impose unlimited overtime working hours. In addition, enterprise unions have usually been willing to cooperate with management to maintain the competitiveness of their companies, including maximum overtime working hours, provided their jobs were maintained. Long working hours, however, have contributed to poor work--life balance among Japanese workers. Although according to some sources it may seem that Japan's working hours are not the longest in comparison to some Anglo-American countries, the data does not include the many hours of "service" (free or unpaid) overtime work in Japan excluded from official statistics (Mouer & Kawanishi 2005: 81–2; Sugimoto 2003: 100–101).

Japan's long working hours have also contributed to the country's low fertility rate, as will be seen later. In extreme cases, long working hours has resulted in *karōshi* (death due to excessively long working hours) and *karō jisatsu* (committing suicide due to the mental illness caused by excessively long working hours) of some Japanese workers (Kawahito 2014; Morioka 2005, 2009: 98–106; North & Morioka 2006; Okumura 1994: 56; Weathers & North 2009; see Figure 5.4). A recent much publicised case was the suicide in December 2015 of Takahashi Matsuri, a young female employee of Japanese media giant Dentsū Corporation, who graduated from Japan's most prestigious University of Tokyo. It was reported that she suffered from mental health problems arising from excessively long working hours, heavy workload and pressure from her seniors (Asahi Shimbun 2016).

Figure 5.4 *Karō jisatsu* in Japan, 1995–2015

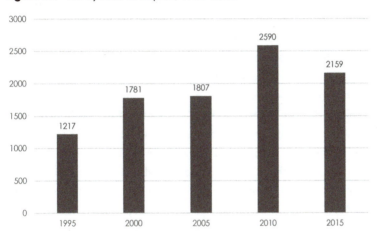

Source: Ministry of Health, Labour and Welfare, *Karōshi nado bōshi taisaku hakusho*, 2016.

Several factors have contributed to the prevalence of long working hours in Japan. There is a cultural explanation of long working hours as a social norm in Japan: work is often based on teamwork and there is peer pressure to work for as long as one's colleagues, otherwise they would need to work even longer hours (Kawanishi 2008; Nemoto 2013). There are also structural and agency factors. As we've already mentioned, Article 36 of the Labour Standards Law failed to ban excessive overtime and instead delegated the decision to employers and unions. Employers were often able to impose unlimited or long overtime by using their greater power over cooperative enterprise unions. Lifetime employment and seniority pay have also provided Japanese workers with an incentive to work for long hours so that they would get promoted and receive higher pay. Even when suffering many hours of unpaid overtime, employees could expect better evaluation from their managers (Mouer & Kawanishi 2005: 76–82; Takahashi 2006). From a macroeconomic perspective, however, unpaid overtime has reduced the number of otherwise available jobs (Tachibanaki 2004: 161).

To tackle the problems of excessively long working hours and *karōshi* and *karō jisatsu*, the current Abe administration has imposed a legal limit on the amount of overtime working hours with the Work-Style Reform. Although this is considered a worker-protective measure, it can also be seen as a measure to enhance labour productivity as well as a measure to improve work-life balance and contribute to improvement in the fertility rate. The Work-Style Reform has imposed a limit of 100 working hours of overtime (each month in the busiest months) and 80 hours (per month on average for any six months) and 720 hours overall per year. This regulation is not only difficult to understand but also allows for more than 80 hours of overtime per month, which many mental health experts consider the *karōshi* line, above which *karōshi* is more likely to happen. Although penalties of less than six months imprisonment and/or a maximum fine of ¥300,000 (about $2,700) are imposed on those who violate this rule, these penalties are relatively light. In addition, there are notable exceptions to this rule, for example, researchers who engage in the development of new technologies and products, medical doctors, construction workers and truck drivers. This lax application of the maximum legal limit on overtime working hours is a consequence of employers' greater strength in the policymaking process. As a result, it is not clear to what extent this legal limit will be effective.

As discussed in Chapter 2, the LDP government has implemented significant labour market deregulation since the late 1990s, mostly in non-regular employment (Imai 2011; Miura 2012; Watanabe 2012, 2014,

2015a). As a result, the percentage of non-regular workers among total workers has increased, while the percentage of regular workers has decreased (see Figures 5.5 and 5.6). Temporary agency work, which was legalized with the enactment of the Temporary Work Agency Law in 1985, was liberalized with the 1999 amendment which banned the use of temporary agency work only in a small number of job categories and economic sectors, including manufacturing. However, the Koizumi administration's 2003 amendment allowed employers in the manufacturing sector to use temporary agency workers. Given the importance of manufacturing in the Japanese economy, this amendment was significant. After the DPJ government had slightly increased the protection of temporary workers by banning so-called "daily temp" (temporary agency work with a duration of less than 30 days) in 2012, the current Abe administration further liberalized the law in a 2015 amendment that allowed employers to use temporary agency work without any time limit as long as employers use different temporary workers every three years. From an employer's perspective, it does not matter who are temporary workers if they can continue to use temporary workers for the same job positions. From an employee's perspective, however, this amendment meant that they would lose a temporary work position every three years unless they are rehired as regular workers or fixed-term workers.

The use of fixed-term contracts has also been deregulated since the late 1990s with an exception of some re-regulation during the DPJ government between 2009 and 2012. Both the 1998 and 2003 amendments to the Labour Standards Law by the LDP administrations were aimed at promoting the use of fixed-term contracts by extending the legal time limit on their use. However, the DPJ government increased the protection of fixed-term workers by enacting the Labour Contract Law in 2012, which stipulated that they are assumed to be employed as regular workers after five years of service. However, this exacerbated the problem of *yatoidome* – the termination of, or refusal to renew, a fixed-term contract – as many employers dismissed fixed-term workers just before their five years was up in order to avoid this legal obligation.

Figure 5.5   Percentage of regular and non-regular workers among total workers in Japan, 2000–2018

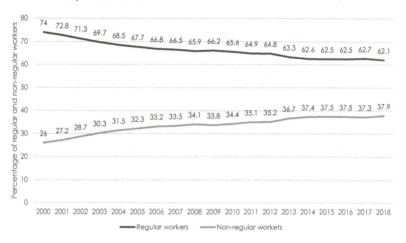

Source: Statistics Bureau, *Labour Force Survey*, 2018.

Figure 5.6   Percentage of part-time, fixed-term and temporary agency workers among total workers in Japan, 2002–18

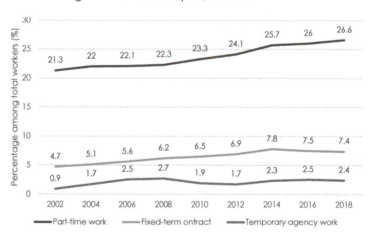

Source: Statistics Bureau, *Labour Force Survey*, 2018.

Part-time work has been re-regulated, rather than deregulated, partly because there has been no legal restriction imposed on the use of part-time work. In Japan, part-time work is more concerned with work status rather than shorter working hours. Indeed, part-time workers may work the same hours as full-time workers, but they are categorized as such only because they were hired as "part-time workers". Although their working hours are typically shorter than those of regular full-time workers, it is common for them to work from 9am to 5pm for example. Most part-time workers are female, and their status as part-time workers is often based on the gender discrimination in the labour market, which will be discussed in the next section. As the working conditions of part-time workers may be as poor as those of temporary workers and their salaries are among the lowest, there were several amendments to the Part-Time Work Law aimed at improving their working conditions, albeit only slightly. For example, the 2007 amendment stipulated that so-called "pseudo" part-time workers, who are permanent part-time workers whose working conditions are the same as those of full-time regular workers in terms of job description, responsibilities, etc., except their job status, should be treated equally as full-time regular workers, including their remuneration. However, the percentage of pseudo part-time workers among all part-time workers is only small – estimated to be 4–5 per cent. The 2014 amendment to the Part-Time Work Law expanded the scope of part-time workers who should be treated equally with full-time regular workers by extending the coverage of equal treatment to "fixed-term" part-time workers whose working conditions are the same.

However, the working conditions of most part-time workers remain poor and precarious. This is partly because many of these workers are middle-aged married female workers who engage in part-time work for the purpose of supplementing the family income. There has always been downward pressure on part-time workers' wages, as the government tax policy and corporate pay rules stipulate favourable treatment of low-paid (female) workers in terms of income tax exemption and deduction. For example, married women whose annual income was less than ¥1.03

million were exempted from paying income tax and the husbands of those spouses were able to claim income tax deduction until recently, when the LDP government raised the income ceiling for these benefits slightly higher to ¥1.5 million. Also, the government tax policy and corporate pay rules assume that most part-time workers are middle-aged married women in a conservative, gender-biased manner. As a result, the working conditions of part-time workers remain poor, as they are supposed to depend on their husbands in the case of job loss. However, the number of male workers who can support their dependents with only their salaries has been decreasing.

The low salaries and precarious working conditions of an increasing number of non-regular workers in Japan, now almost 40 per cent of the total work force, have contributed to deflation and stagnant economic growth due to their low amount of spending. The Abe administration's Work-Style Reform, which stipulated equal treatment between regular and non-regular workers, including equal pay for equal work, is aimed at increasing the spending power of non-regular workers rather than improving their working conditions per se. In fact, there is no penalty against employers' violation of equal treatment between regular and non-regular workers, in contrast to infringement of the legal limit on overtime working hours introduced in the same Work-Style Reform. The equal treatment provision is based on administrative guidance issued by the Ministry of Health, Labour and Welfare and so is not expected to be effective. This is partly because the policy measure is mostly about economic growth rather than the protection of non-regular workers.

As for industrial relations, they were originally conflict-ridden after the end of the Second World War during the initiation of the US occupation, when labour unions were legalized for the first time in Japanese history. Although public-sector unions were deprived of the right to strike by the US occupation authority during the anti-communist "reverse course" with the intensification of the Cold War, private-sector unions continued to engage in strikes frequently until their defeat in the Mitsui Miike Mine strike in 1960. It was the largest-scale strike conducted by private-sector unions, and their defeat signified the end of large-scale strikes by private-sector unions (Nishinarita 1998: 203, 206). After this incident, Japanese labour unions led by enterprise unions in the internationally competitive sectors of automobiles and electronics achieved labour–management consensus and have since maintained mostly cooperative industrial relations with management (Nishinarita 1998: 197). With the failure of the national railway strike in 1975, the International Metal Federation of Japan Council (IMF-JC) of the Dōmei (Japan Confederation of Labour), comprised of Japan's internationally competitive sectors such as automobile and electronics, assumed the leading role in Japan's labour movement and strengthened unions' cooperation with management to compete with foreign companies and cope with the lower economic growth caused by the oil crisis in 1974 (Kume 1998, 2005). As a result, the number of strikes in Japan decreased significantly (see Figure 5.7). Japanese labour unions led by the two national confederations of Sōhyō (General Council of Trade Unions of Japan) and Dōmei were transformed against a background of the continued strength of private-sector

Figure 5.7 Number of strikes in Japan, 1960–2015

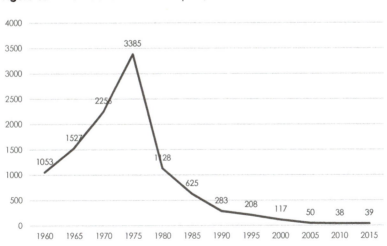

Source: Ministry of Health, Labour and Welfare, *Labour Dispute Survey*, 2016.

unions in the competitive industrial sectors. In the end, Rengō (Japanese Trade Union Confederation) was formed in 1989 with the incorporation of public-sector unions of Sōhyō into the private-sector Rengō.

Rengō has essentially been a representative of the interests of regular workers in large companies. As a result, the protection of their jobs has been its most important mission. However, Rengō, as the largest national confederation in Japan, has also had to show concern for poor and deteriorating working conditions of not only non-regular workers but also an increasing number of regular workers against a background of severe economic pressure after the collapse of the bubble economy and intensified international competition from neighbouring Asian countries. Rengō has not been able to simply ignore the increasing number of poorly paid non-regular workers with unstable jobs since the implementation of labour market deregulation in the late 1990s. In the policymaking process related to non-regular work, such as temporary agency work and fixed-term contracts, Rengō has sought to increase the job protection of non-regular workers against employers' attempts to further deregulate non-regular employment. However, Rengō's opposition to employers' policy proposals has often been ineffective, as the muscle of unions has become smaller due to the decline in union density (the percentage of union members among total workers) and their reduced access to the government policymaking. Japan's union density has been declining for a long time and remain low (see Figure 5.8). As for labour policymaking, the newly established Cabinet councils, such as the Deregulation Committee, removed labour unions from their membership after the launch of the Koizumi administration in 2001 (Watanabe 2012, 2014, 2015a).

In contrast to mainstream unions such as enterprise unions, regional or local unions such as community and general unions, which any individual workers can join irrespective of their company affiliation, remain eager to improve the working conditions of individual workers. Those individually-affiliated unions have empowered hitherto unorganized regular workers in SMEs and non-regular workers in precarious positions by organizing and assisting them in labour disputes with employers

Figure 5.8   Union density in Japan, 1990–2015

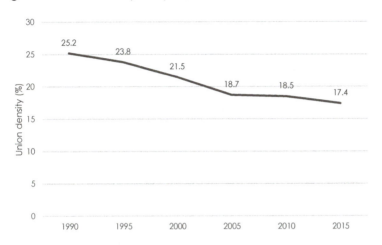

Source: Ministry of Health, Labour and Welfare, *Basic Survey on Labour Unions*, 2016.

(Watanabe 2015b, 2018b). Some of these unions have formed a coalition with social movement NGOs (called "social movement unionism") and actively engaged in political actions by holding meetings with the DPJ and Communist Party politicians in the Diet and making policy requests to bureaucrats in ministries such as the MHLW. However, individually-affiliated unions have struggled to retain members, as their members tend to leave unions once their labour disputes with employers are resolved. As a result, the human and financial resources of those unions remain too small to revitalize the labour movement significantly.

GENDER DISCRIMINATION IN THE JAPANESE LABOUR MARKET

Significant gender discrimination exists in the Japanese labour market. While gender discrimination in the labour market exists in all countries and the Japanese situation may be improving to some extent in some areas, gender discrimination in the Japanese labour market is more serious than in many other industrialized countries. This section will first identify some indicators of gender discrimination such as gender wage gaps, the percentage of women in managerial positions, women's labour market participation and women's career course. It will then discuss how we might explain such discrimination by examining agency (employers' and employees' incentives to engage in or endure gender discrimination), structure (public policies such as the Equal Employment Opportunity Law, employment practices and industrial relations) and social norms that supports the traditional understanding of gender roles.

Among ten selected countries of the OECD (Japan, South Korea, the US, the UK, France, Germany, Sweden, Italy, Spain and Poland), the gender wage gap (median earnings, full-time employees) in Japan is the second largest (24.5%) after South Korea (34.6%) according to OECD data (see Figure 5.9). In Japan, female workers only receive three quarters of male workers' wages. The three best performers with the narrowest wage gap are Italy (5.6%), Poland (9.4%) and France (9.9%), with all these countries having a gender wage gap of less than 10 per cent. As for the female share of managers (all ages), Japan's percentage is the second lowest (12.4%), which is only better than South Korea (10.5%) according to

Figure 5.9 Gender wage gap, selected countries, 2017

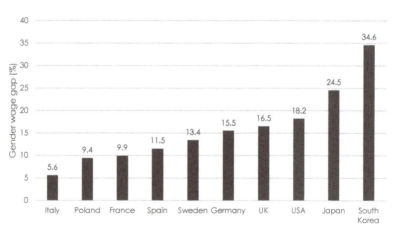

Source: OECD Data, 2017 or the latest available.

the OECD data (see Figure 5.10). The current Abe administration aims to raise this to 30 per cent by 2020 but this is overly ambitious. The three top performers in this respect are the US (43.4%), Poland (40.2%) and Sweden (39.5%).

Figure 5.10 Women in managerial positions, selected countries (Women's share of employment in managerial jobs) 2017

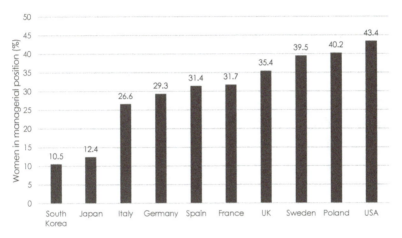

Source: OECD Data, 2017 or the latest available.

Another indicator of gender discrimination in the Japanese labour market is women's labour market participation rates. As seen in Figure 5.11, mapping Japanese (and Korean) women's labour market participation over a working lifetime produces an M-shaped curve. In contrast, labour market participation rates of Swedish and German women are characterized by a reverse U shape. This would indicate that, while Swedish and German women continue to work after marriage or childbirth (or use maternity leave and then come back to workplace), many Japanese and Korean women quit, spend a few years taking care of children full time, and then return to the labour market as low-paid part-time workers to contribute to the family income. We shall examine the reasons for this phenomenon later. We can also see, however, from Figure 5.12, that the Japanese curve has become flatter in recent years. This suggests that there are more women who continue working at the time of marriage or childbirth (by taking maternity leave) or that some women simply forsake having a child to continue working. If women leave work, they are likely to do so at a later stage of their career.

Figure 5.11 Female labour force participation rate by age, selected countries, 2017

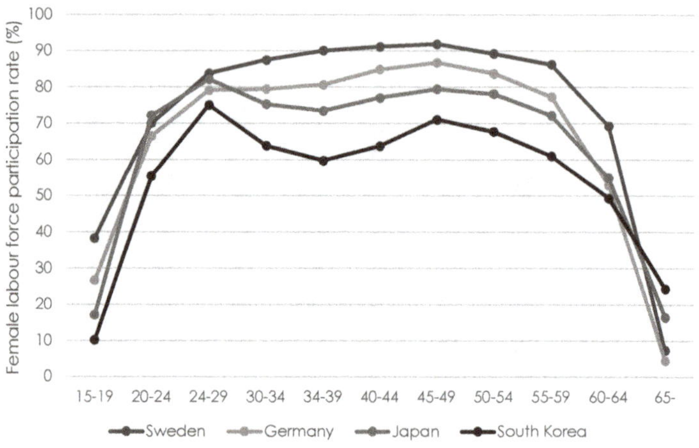

Source: Gender Equality Bureau, Cabinet Office, *Danjo kyōdō sankaku hakusho*, 2018.

A final indicator of gender discrimination is that most female university graduates join a company on its "assistant" track (*ippan shoku*) in the dual career track system, which was introduced by large Japanese companies soon after the enactment of the Equal Employment Opportunity Law (EEOL) in 1985. Whereas, most male university graduates enter on the "management" track (*sōgō shoku*), in which they can expect promotion. Although the dual career track system may look gender discriminatory, Japanese employers claim that it is not so because women workers are offered a choice between the management and assistant tracks when they first enter the company. However, given the long working hours of workers on the management track, Japanese women, more interested in a good

Figure 5.12 Female labour force participation rate by age in Japan, 1997 and 2017

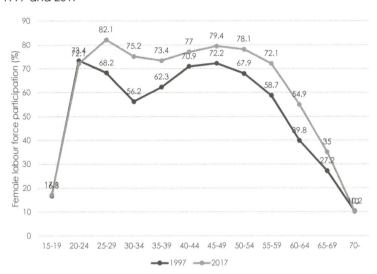

Source: Gender Equality Bureau, Cabinet Office, *Danjo kyōdō sankaku hakusho*, 2018.

work-life balance than career progression, choose the assistant track, whether voluntarily or involuntarily (Lam 1992, 1993: 212–15).

We can use three different analytical perspectives – agency, structure and ideas – to explain the causes of gender discrimination in the Japanese labour market. By agency, we mean the actions taken by relevant actors, such as employers and female employees, based on the incentives provided to them. For example, from the demand side of labour, employers may discriminate against female workers from a human capital perspective based on "statistical discrimination" (Osawa 1999: 209–10). As Japanese women tend to leave work when they marry or have children, at least statistically, either because of the pressure from employers and/or colleagues or because of their intention to avoid the dual burden of work and childcare, employers tend to assume that female workers will leave in those situations even if some female workers intend to continue in their job. As a result, employers tend to think it would be a waste of resources from a human capital perspective to invest in the skill development of female workers and so treat them as inferior workers such as non-regular workers or regular workers in the "assistant" track. The economist Gary Becker used the concept of "comparative advantage" to explain the gender division of labour claiming that if men are better at earning money in the labour market and women are better at taking care of the home and children, then it makes sense for men to focus on company work and women to focus on housework as they have comparative advantage in those works respectively (Becker 1981). This conservative reasoning of the gender division of labour has been much criticized but remains influential.

Another agency perspective emphasizes the importance for employers to maintain a flexible and low-cost workforce in case of economic downturns or to survive in a time of intensified international competition (Watanabe 2012, 2014, 2015a). In this economic context, ensuring gender-equal opportunities that may prolong women's career continuity and increase the number of female employees with job security would not only increase labour costs but also reduce employment flexibility by losing low-cost peripheral workers. Most employers, or those in management positions, in Japanese companies are men and they tend to assign women workers to inferior positions in terms of job security and pay. As a result, gender discrimination in the labour market is likely to be maintained.

Some researchers emphasize the agency of female workers from a supply-side perspective to explain the existence of gender discrimination in the labour market. Among the most controversial is Katherine Hakim's argument that women workers choose and endure gender discrimination "voluntarily" in order to strike a better work-life balance (Hakim 1995). Hakim argues that it would be a mistake to assume that all women workers want to work as men do, as some women prefer to avoid the dual shift of hard work at the company and care work at home and so voluntarily choose inferior positions. From this perspective, it is not necessarily employers that discriminate against female workers but women workers themselves that help create different treatment of employees based on gender. However, it is possible to criticize this view by questioning if women really choose inferior job positions voluntarily. In the context of conservative, gender-based Japanese society, it would be extremely difficult for women to work as regular workers, as not only do they need to work for long hours but they would also have the main responsibility for housework such as child and elderly care. Those male regular workers under lifetime employment hardly have time to share such housework. In this situation, women's choice might better be described as "forced" or involuntary rather than voluntary (Kumazawa 2000: 134–6).

Gender discrimination in the Japanese labour market can also be explained structurally by focusing on the impact of public policy, employment practices and industrial relations. The Japanese government enacted the Equal Employment Opportunity Law (EEOL) in 1985 to prohibit gender discrimination in the labour market in terms of job recruitment, assignment, promotion, training, corporate welfare, employment status, dismissal and so on (EEOL, Articles 5 and 6). The EEOL originally banned only direct discrimination but the law was strengthened by several amendments, such as those in 2006 and 2013 which banned "indirect" discrimination in some cases. Indirect discrimination includes, according to the ordinances of the Ministry of Health, Labour and Welfare, specifying that new employees must satisfy certain conditions in terms of height, weight and body strength. For example, since the number of Japanese women taller than 170 cm is quite small, the recruitment method that stipulates that new employees must be 170 cm or taller could be considered as indirect discrimination, although it does not directly say that women are unwanted. However, the EEOL remains unsatisfactory – its definition of indirect discrimination is still narrow in scope and it does not penalize employers who violate its stipulations but only encourages employers to make efforts to observe them.

The EEOL has also exacerbated gender discrimination in the Japanese labour market by institutionalizing the so-called "dual career track system", if unintentionally. After the EEOL was enacted in 1985, some employers, especially those in large companies, introduced two career tracks: the "management" track (*sōgō shoku*) and the "assistant" track (*ippan shoku*). Employees on the management track can expect career promotion to managerial positions with an annual increase in their salaries and benefits. Those employees on the "assistant" track, however, remain in subordinate positions, often engaged in routine mundane tasks, and cannot expect promotion or any significant increase in their salaries and other benefits. In most cases, almost 100 per cent of male employees join the company on the management track and almost all female employees enter on the assistant track (Lam 1992: 128–33; 1993: 212–15). For example, in the case of one of the largest Japanese multinational trading companies where the author used to work, only one out of more than 150 or 200 female university graduates entered the management track each year. Japanese employers have maintained, however, that the dual career track is not a discriminatory measure, as new female employees are given the opportunity to choose the management track rather than the assistant track when they enter the company. This may be true. However, as already mentioned, both the excessive work commitment and long working hours required from full-time regular workers in the management track prompt most women to choose the assistant track, especially those who aspire to strike a healthier work–life balance. It is ironical, therefore, that the EEOL, which is aimed at eliminating gender discrimination in the labour market, has unintentionally contributed to its institutionalization in the form of the dual career track system.

Japan's tax and social security system and corporate welfare provision have also affected women's position in the labour market negatively (Houseman & Osawa 2003: 199; Osawa 2009: 171–3). They have provided female workers with an incentive to remain in low-paid jobs that prevent them from being promoted. As seen in Chapter 2, Japanese income tax law stipulates that income tax becomes payable when annual income reaches ¥1.5 million (around $13,600 at current exchange rates) and that if a worker earns less than the tax threshold and is married, the worker's spouse is also entitled to a deduction in their income tax. There are similar rules in the case of the payment of pension premiums and national health insurance tax (with a ceiling of ¥1.3 million) with exemption for female workers as the spouse of their working husband. In the case of corporate welfare such as family allowance, male workers are entitled to these benefits only when the annual income of their spouse is less than ¥1.03 million. These policies and welfare system have provided Japanese female workers with an incentive to remain as low-paid workers, most typically middle-aged part-time workers, and have put them in an inferior position in the labour market, just as the dual career track system has done.

In addition, Japan's employment practice based on lifetime employment and seniority-based pay and promotion has contributed to the gender discrimination in the labour market. In order to maintain a job and benefit from a pay and promotion system based on seniority, male Japanese workers under lifetime employment have been committed to working for very long hours and do not have the time left for childcare. This has made it very difficult for married female workers burdened with heavy childcare duties to do anything other than take a job on the assistant track (when they work full-time) or undertake non-regular employment such as part-time work, which provides for a better work-life balance. This feature of Japanese employment has contributed to the institutionalization of women workers' lower position in the labour market as well as the under-utilization of the female workforce in Japan.

Japan's industrial relations have also contributed to gender discrimination and female workers' inferior positions in the labour market. The main actors in Japan's industrial relations are employers and members of enterprise unions. The basic unit of Japanese unions is the enterprise union in contrast to continental Europe, where the basic unit is the industry-wide trade union. As the existence of enterprise unions depends on the survival of their companies, enterprise unions have a strong incentive to cooperate with management so that their companies can remain competitive and survive and the jobs of their union members as regular workers are protected. As enterprise unions share the employers' perspective, equal employment opportunities for female workers are seen as negatively affecting companies' cost performance and competitiveness. In addition, enterprise unions have been dominated by male workers and women's working conditions have not been a priority. While national confederations such as Rengō have sought to represent the interests of all workers based on the concept of labour solidarity at least more than enterprise unions, it often remains a mere lip service to female union members. Instead, Rengō has focused on the protection of the vested interests of male regular workers in large companies as the core members of their unions. This attitude of Japanese labour unions has hardly contributed to the improvement of women's working conditions in the labour market.

Finally, Japan's social and cultural norms have contributed to gender discrimination in the labour market (Rosenbluth 2007: 5–7). In Japan, it remains a well-entrenched conservative view that women are the primary care providers in the domestic family sphere and are not supposed to engage in employment as full-time workers. Interestingly, a large percentage of Japanese women themselves still share this gender-based conservative social norm. According to a public opinion survey conducted by the Gender Equality Bureau of Cabinet Office in 2014, 46.5 per cent of Japanese men and 43.2 per cent of Japanese women agreed with the statement "Husbands should work outside, and wives should stay at home to take care of children". Although the percentage of women who disagreed was higher (51.6%), more than 40 per cent of Japanese women shared this view while the percentage of men who agreed and disagreed was the same at 46.5 percent. Japanese society remains based on the male breadwinner model, where men are typically supposed to work in the labour market as principal workers and women are typically supposed to be either full-time housewives or, if in employment, part-time workers who provide a supplementary income to the family budget.

Gender discrimination in the Japanese labour market can therefore be explained from the perspectives of agency (employers' and employees' incentives), structure (public policy, employment practices and industrial relations) and social norms based on conservative, gender-based ideas. In international comparison, the factors identified from a structural or social norm perspective may be a little more distinctive or peculiar to the Japanese situation than those identified from an agency perspective. However, no single perspective can fully explain the existence of gender discrimination in the Japanese labour market.

LABOUR MARKET DUALISM AND DIVERSIFICATION

Labour market dualism in Japan can be seen in the difference between regular and non-regular employment (see Chapter 2 for other examples of economic dualism including the difference between large companies and SMEs). Labour market dualism is said to arise because the core members of labour unions, i.e. regular workers (in large companies), protect their jobs as insiders at the cost of jobs of non-regular workers as outsiders by cooperating with employers (Emmenegger *et al.* 2012; Emmenegger 2015; Palier & Thelen 2010; Rueda 2007; Thelen 2009, 2014; Thelen & Kume 1999, 2006). According to this view, regular workers (in large companies) as insiders enjoy better working conditions in that their jobs are better protected, their salaries are higher, and they receive better social welfare provision such as company pensions and health insurance. Whereas, non-regular workers as outsiders suffer from poor working conditions in that their jobs are less protected, their salaries are lower, and they receive meager social welfare and so on. Although this view correctly identifies several characteristics that are common among regular workers and non-regular workers, it misses the recent changes in regular employment and the deteriorating working conditions of regular workers, especially in Japan (Watanabe 2018a).

As mentioned above, the LDP government has implemented significant labour market deregulation since the late 1990s, mostly in non-regular employment such as temporary agency work and fixed-term contracts (Watanabe 2012, 2014, 2015a). However, the deregulation of non-regular employment has deteriorated the working conditions of regular workers by making it easier for employers to use non-regular workers instead of regular workers not only in the service sectors but also in the manufacturing sectors (Imai 2011: 163). An increasing number of non-regular workers who engage in jobs previously performed by regular workers has threatened jobs of regular workers by enabling employers to replace them with cheaper non-regular workers in the case of their reluctance to work in poorer conditions. In fact, the number of regular workers aged 15-24 has decreased since the 1990s, in particular due to university graduates being hired as non-regular workers rather than as regular workers in times of economic stagnation (Goka 1999: 83; Gotō 2011: 9–12; see Figure 5.1). As a result, working conditions of regular workers have deteriorated, as we have seen in the work load (cf. *karōshi* and *karō jisatsu*) and in the stagnant wages since the mid-1990s (with little increase in the gap between regular and non-regular workers' wages), which is contrary to the dualism perspective that assumes protected work conditions for regular workers (see Figures 5.2 and 5.3). Despite the official stance of Rengō and some industrial federations of opposition to the greater use of non-regular workers by employers, enterprise unions in competitive sectors have not opposed it. They consider non-regular workers as a necessary buffer for coping with economic fluctuations and maintaining business competitiveness and have been reluctant to organize an increasing number of non-regular workers. As a result, union density has declined further (Mouer & Kawanishi 2005: 127). In this situation, national organizations such as Rengō and industrial federations in the service sectors, where there are many non-regular workers, have begun to encourage enterprise unions to organize non-regular workers and attempt to reduce an insider-outsider gap. However, the progress has to date been slow.

As we have seen, in addition to non-regular employment, the LDP government also implemented deregulation of regular employment with the 1998 and 2003 amendments to the Labour Standards Law and most recently with the enactment of the Work-Style Reform in 2018, which completely exempted a certain category of workers ("highly professional") from working-time regulations. These deregulation initiatives – the expansion of discretionary work and now the introduction of highly professional work – has contributed to excessively long working hours of those workers without enough autonomy in the management of their work and exacerbated their working conditions. The real situation in Japan is more complex than the picture of good working conditions for regular workers presented by the labour market dualism perspective.

The LDP government has also discussed the idea of relaxing rules on dismissal of regular workers. According to Article 16 of the Labour Standards Law, employers cannot dismiss employees without socially acceptable reasons. This means that employers must satisfy at least one of the four conditions stipulated by legal precedents, which are related to employees' incapacity, their failure to obey company rules, business difficulties and employee redundancy, and other reasons that necessitate employers to dismiss employees. Most recently, the current Abe administration proposed the idea of fiduciary compensation in the case of unfair dismissal. The Regulatory Reform Council and the newly established Industrial Competitiveness Council were eager to relax the dismissal rule so that workers in inefficient and declining industrial sectors could move to new or efficient industrial sectors and contribute to economic growth, which remains the current Abe administration's top priority. For this purpose, the Industrial Competitiveness Council proposed the introduction of fiduciary compensation in the case of unfair dismissal, first in the newly established "strategic special economic zones" (*senyaku tokku*) and then nationwide (Asahi Shimbun 2015; Industrial Competitiveness Council 2013a, 2013b; Nishitani 2014: 18–21; Watanabe 2018a). Although the current Abe administration quietly withdrew the proposal to relax the dismissal rule in order to prioritize other measures to deregulate regular employment (such as the introduction of highly professional work), employer associations may strengthen their demand for more flexible regular employment in the future, depending on the economic situation.

The current Abe administration has also aimed to diversify regular employment by increasing the number of "semi-regular" workers (*gentei seishain*). Semi-regular workers are different from core regular workers under lifetime employment arrangements in that they can choose a job location and are not assigned to any other location against their will. Their job responsibilities are also limited unlike core regular workers whose job responsibilities are unlimited. Semi-regular workers are regular workers in status, but their wages are lower than those of core regular workers although higher than those of non-regular workers. Employment protection of semi-regular workers is not as secure as it is for core regular workers either (Morioka 2015: 141–4). In this sense, the increased use of semi-regular work may be considered as the diversification of regular employment and the labour market, rather than dualization. Although some companies have already been using semi-regular workers to both improve work-life balance and increase the employment of female workers, the current Abe administration has attempted to promote the use of semi-regular workers as part of its economic growth strategy through more flexible regular employment (see Industrial Competitiveness Council 2013c for Prime Minister Abe's intention to promote semi-regular work and eliminate the dual labour market). Critics of this measure argue, however, that the greater use of semi-regular workers is nothing more than a way to continue using female regular workers more cheaply and facilitate easier dismissal, as the jobs of semi-regular workers are not protected as much as those of regular workers under lifetime employment arrangements.

The reasons why Japanese labour unions have allowed the current Abe administration to introduce these measures to deregulate regular employment may be explained by the weakening power of labour unions (Korpi 1983, 2006; Watanabe 2014, 2018a). First, labour unions lost access to the policymaking process in Cabinet councils such as the Regulatory Reform Council and the Industrial Competitiveness Council (Miura 2012; Watanabe 2014, 2015a). The LDP government established Cabinet councils to expedite the policymaking process in a top-down manner by allowing those councils to monopolize agenda-setting powers. Although the advisory councils of the Ministry of Health, Labour and Welfare (MHLW) still exist and play an important role in labour policymaking based on tripartite decision making among employers, unions and the bureaucrats of the MHLW, their policymaking power has been undermined to some extent with the establishment of Cabinet councils. This has also affected the political influence of labour unions negatively, as they do not have policymaking access to Cabinet councils such as the Regulatory Reform Council.

In addition to unions' reduced access to government policymaking, declining union density has weakened their power to resist deregulation of regular employment by reducing their human and financial resources. Union density in Japan has been declining, especially since the government's implementation of labour market deregulation in the late 1990s (see Figure 5.8). Against this background, Rengō and some industrial federations have made efforts to organize regular workers in SMEs and non-regular workers, but with limited success, as enterprise unions in general and the industrial federations in competitive sectors, such as JC-Metal, have been uninterested and have made little effort to organize those workers (Suzuki 2012: 75). As we have seen, these unions have been more interested in maintaining cooperative industrial relations with employers so as not to weaken the productivity and competitiveness of their companies rather than fighting against employers by conducting strikes based on class solidarity (Suzuki 2012: 79, 86; see Figure 5.7 for the decreasing number of strikes since 1975). However, the declining union density as a result has negatively affected unions' capacity to organize and mobilize workers.

Japanese unions have also suffered from the conflicts of interest brought about by their different preferences for labour market flexibility, despite achieving a higher level of organizational unity after the establishment of the largest national union confederation Rengō in 1989. Conflicts of interest weakened the political power of unions and made it more difficult to resist government proposals to deregulate regular employment. Enterprise unions, which have mostly represented the interests of regular workers in large companies rather than promoting general class interests and which have tended towards cross-class alliance with employers rather than maintaining class solidarity, control a large amount of financial resources in comparison to Rengō, as enterprise unions collect union fees directly from their members and only a small percentage of these fees are allocated to industrial federations and then Rengō (Suzuki 2006: 293). The human resources of Rengō are also relatively small in comparison to those of industrial federations and enterprise unions (Nakamura & Miura 2005: 193). As a result, Rengō has not been able to unify the different positions of its affiliated enterprise unions and industrial federations and has not been able to prevent the LDP government from introducing measures to deregulate regular employment.

Due to the reduced access to policymaking, declining union density, insufficient capacity to organize and mobilize workers, and the conflicts of interest in labour market flexibility, the power of unions has declined and the power balance between unions and employers has shifted towards the latter. The economic interests of employers have been well represented by the Cabinet councils and they have been able to maintain institutionalized access to policy-making in Cabinet councils in contrast to labour unions, which lost such access after the inauguration of the neoliberal Koizumi administration (Watanabe 2012, 2014, 2015a). Contrary to the theoretical expectation based on a dualism perspective, Japanese employers and the LDP government have attempted to promote deregulation of not only non-regular employment but also regular employment. Faced with tougher international competition, Japanese employers have been eager to enhance their competitiveness by lowering labour costs and increasing employment flexibility with a narrower scope of regular workers under lifetime employment. The current Abe administration also has been eager to achieve economic growth with its Abenomics by enhancing labour productivity through deregulation.

As a result of deregulation and more flexible use of regular employment, the Japanese labour market has diversified, albeit not as extensively deregulated as liberal market economies such as the United States. A greater diversity can be identified in the Japanese labour market that includes a shrinking number of "core" regular workers, who are protected under lifetime employment but increasingly suffer from deteriorated working conditions; "professional" regular workers, who are supposed to have job discretion, if not in practice, and work under deregulated working-time rules without receiving overtime pay; "peripheral" regular workers, who have become more vulnerable to employers' neoliberal offensives on job protection and do not benefit from seniority-based pay despite their status as regular workers; "semi"-regular workers mentioned above; and non-regular workers, whose working conditions remain precarious (Watanabe 2018a: 580, 592). Although dualism between regular and non-regular employment still exists, the Japanese labour market has become more diverse rather than remain dualistic. Not only has the scope of regular workers under lifetime employment been shrinking but also an increasing number of regular workers have suffered from poorer working conditions in more flexible regular employment.

POOR WORKING CONDITIONS AND UNION RESPONSE

Labour market deregulation since the later 1990s has contributed to poorer working conditions of Japanese workers. The working conditions of non-regular workers (and regular workers in SMEs) are generally poor in terms of job security, pay, social insurance such as pension, and fringe benefits such as family allowance. As a result of 2015 legislation, temporary agency workers may lose their job every three years unless they are rehired as regular workers or fixed-term workers, which given employers' general inclination to maintain low labour costs, is not guaranteed.

A similar situation of work precarity exists for fixed-term workers. For them, renewals of a fixed-term contract are a matter of survival. Non-renewal or termination of a fixed-term contract (*yatoidome*) without good reason has become a controversial issue in Japan with employees suing their companies for unreasonable *yatoidome*. As we have seen, the DPJ government between 2009 and 2012 increased the protection of fixed-term workers by enacting the Labour Contract Law, which requires employers to have objective reasons for terminating a fixed-term contract and prohibits unreasonable discriminatory treatment between fixed-term workers and regular workers. Perhaps the most controversial provision (article 18) stipulates that an employer is deemed to have given consent to an employee's request to convert his or her work from a fixed-term contract to a regular full-time contract once the employee has been in the job for five years and makes such a request. This has given rise to *yatoidome* by employers who were eager to avoid hiring these workers as regular workers to contain labour costs. Given the imbalance of power between employers and fixed-term workers and employers' keenness to avoid the law, a large number of fixed-term workers have been fired ahead of completing their five years. This demonstrates the difficulty of ensuring the protection of non-regular workers even by a government that is sympathetic to their precarious working conditions.

Non-regular workers are also subject to a lower level of pay. Male non-regular workers receive only around 70 per cent of the salaries of male regular workers, and female non-regular workers receive lower than 50 per cent of the salaries of male regular workers. There is hardly any incentive for employers to raise the wages of non-regular workers unless it may contribute to an increase in labour productivity. At times of economic stagnation or hardship, however, employers cannot afford to raise the wages of non-regular workers and instead are likely to seek lower labour costs by increasing the use of non-regular workers. Another reason for the low wages of non-regular workers is the low minimum wages in Japan in international comparison. As of October 2019, the average minimum wage in Japan is only around ¥900 per hour (equivalent to around $8) and even the highest minimum wage in the Tokyo prefecture is around ¥1,000 (minimum wages in Japan are set at the prefectural level). As non-regular workers' wages are paid on an hourly rate in contrast to regular workers' wages on a monthly basis, the level of the minimum wages directly affects non-regular workers' wages. Despite the efforts of major Japanese unions to raise the minimum wage to at least ¥1,000 nationwide, the levels of Japan's minimum wage remain low and continue to contribute to the low wages of non-regular workers.

The "working poor" has become a serious concern in Japan, especially since the global financial crisis when their existence became more visible

(Osawa 2010; Osawa, Kim & Kingston 2013). The definition of working poor depends on how we first define "work" and whether the unit of analysis is individuals or households (Goishi 2011: 119–25; Iwai *et al.* 2009; Michinaka 2009). In Japan, however, working poor often means those individual workers whose annual income is less than ¥2 million (about $18,000). The annual income of the working poor is similar to, or sometimes even lower than, the amount of benefits for those who receive social (public) assistance. The percentage of the working poor ranges from around 16 per cent to 25 per cent of total working population, depending on the statistics we use. According to the 2017 data of the Ministry of Internal Affairs and Communications, 75 per cent of non-regular workers were working poor with an annual income of less than ¥2 million and in the case of female non-regular workers, the percentage was 83 per cent (Asahi Shimbun 2019c). The percentage of working poor has increased due to the implementation of labour market deregulation and an increase in the number of non-regular workers since the 1990s. Although being working poor may not necessarily mean being in a precarious position in the case of low-paid part-time workers who have somebody else to depend on (typically middle-aged female part-time workers who are low paid but have husbands who are high-income regular workers), it does become highly precarious in the case of a sole low-income earner with dependants who do not earn any income or who earn only a small amount of income. Although being a different metric from the working poor, Japan's relative poverty rate (the percentage of those who are below the poverty line defined as the annual income of 50 per cent of the national median income) is among the highest in OECD countries, as we saw in Chapter 3, despite the myth of Japan as a middle-class society.

Japanese non-regular workers are also disadvantaged in terms of social insurance such as pension and health insurance. Given that the amount of pension a person may receive depends on how much salary they have earned, it is no surprise that non-regular workers on low salaries are disadvantaged. In addition, while a high percentage of regular workers (92.9%) are members of corporate pension schemes, which is more generous than the national state pension, the percentage of non-regular workers who are members of such company schemes is much lower, especially part-time workers (32.8% of part-time workers and 38.6% of part-time workers who are entitled to a corporate pension as a spouse of their higher-income partner). The same situation applies to national health insurance. While regular workers (in large companies) and their spouses are entitled to national health insurance at a favourable rate (only paying a fee of 10 per cent of actual costs in hospitals, dentists and so on), non-regular workers who are not members of a corporate health insurance association pay a fee of 30 per cent of actual costs. Non-regular workers are also disadvantaged in terms of fringe benefits, being much less likely to receive family allowance or company day-care services than regular workers in large companies.

Japan has a relatively low level of social safety net and this has exacerbated the already precarious working conditions of non-regular workers. The entitlement conditions for unemployment insurance are rather strict, although they have been relaxed recently. Those seeking unemployment benefits need to prove that they used to work at least 20 hours per week before they left their job or were dismissed. They also needed to prove that they had been in employment for at least a year (6 months in some cases) before the DPJ government relaxed this regulation to 31 days with the 2010 amendment to the Employment Security Law. However, even with this relaxation, there remain many non-regular workers who cannot satisfy these conditions and are not entitled to unemployment insurance if they lose their job (Hommerich 2012: 218–19). Even when workers are entitled to unemployment insurance, the level of pay is usually low, and they are covered only for a short period between 90 and 360 days. When workers are considered to quit voluntarily (even as a result of harassment by employers, for example), workers are only entitled to unemployment benefit for 90 days.

One of the significant problems with Japan's welfare system is that there is no safety net once unemployment insurance has run out unless benefit seekers are entitled to social (public) assistance. This situation is quite different from some European countries where unemployment assistance is available as the second safety net which covers the period after the expiry of unemployment insurance. Once the period of unemployment insurance expires, the only safety net available in Japan is social (public) assistance, which is aimed at helping very poor individuals and families. In addition, the entitlement conditions for social (public) assistance are punitive, such as no personal savings or household assets. Once workers lose their job, which is more likely to happen to non-regular works than regular workers, and once unemployment insurance expires if they are entitled to it, they are often at risk of becoming homeless.

LOW FERTILITY RATE

Japan's fertility rate remains low at around 1.4 children per woman. A fertility rate of around 2.1 is considered necessary for a country to maintain its population and Japan's fertility rate is far below this. With a fertility rate of 1.4, Japan has a declining population. With fewer children being born and a smaller working-age labour force supporting an increasing non-productive aging population, it will become more difficult for the country to sustain its social welfare system such as its national state pension and its economic power may decline. Despite the Japanese government implementing measures to help increase the fertility rate, Japan's fertility rate remains low. This section will examine why these measures have proved so difficult, but first it aims to identify the relationship (or possible correlation) between the female labour force participation rate and the fertility rate and also the relationship between work-life balance and the fertility rate from an international comparative perspective.

When we look at the relationship between women's labour force participation (women aged 15 and older) and fertility, it seems that there is no clear relationship or correlation (see Figure 5.13 for the fertility rates of selected countries and Figure 5.14 for women's labour force participation rates, which are the percentages of working women among the total women's population). Both "negative" and "positive" correlations can be identified, given the time constraint on working women who also want to raise children, on the one hand, and working women's greater capacity to spend money on childcare, on the other hand. If we look at some countries with higher fertility rates such as Sweden and the US and some other countries with lower fertility rates such as Italy and Japan, we can see a positive correlation between women's labour force participation rate and the fertility rate, meaning the higher the percentage of working women, the higher the fertility rate. However, we can also see examples where this isn't the case. For example, France has the highest fertility rate of 1.96 among the selected countries but a relatively low female labour force participation rate of 50.47 per cent. Similarly, despite a relatively high female labour force participation rate at 55.07 per cent, which is higher than France, Germany's fertility rate is 1.5, which is lower than the fertility rate of France. Although labour market participation would enable women to have greater financial capacity to have children, the findings above suggest that there are several other factors that may affect the fertility rate.

Figure 5.13 Fertility rate, selected countries, 2016

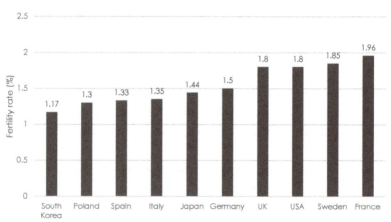

Source: World Bank Data (2019).

Figure 5.14 Female labour force participation rate (age 15+), selected countries, 2016

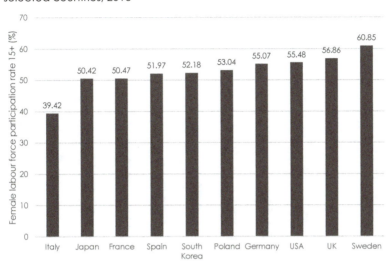

Source: World Bank Data (2019).

It also seems that there is no clear correlation between either work-ing hours or work-life balance and the fertility rate (see Figures 5.15 and 5.16). While countries such as Japan and South Korea that have a high percentage of employees who work more than 50 hours per week and have poor work-life balance have some of the lowest fertility rates, the US and the UK have relatively higher fertility rates despite also having relatively long working hours and poor work-life balance. In contrast, the southern European countries of Italy and Spain have a low fertility rate despite hav-ing a low percentage of employees who work for long hours and having a good work-life balance. As in the case of women's labour force partic-ipation rate, it seems that working hours or work-life balance alone does not determine a country's fertility rate although despite a lack of decisive impact, these factors – essentially time and money – are likely to affect fertility rates.

Figure 5.15 Percentage of employees working 50+ hours per week, selected countries, 2018

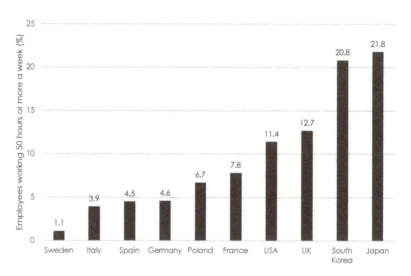

Source: OECD Better Life Index, 2018 or the latest available.

Figure 5.16 Work–life balance index, selected countries, 2018

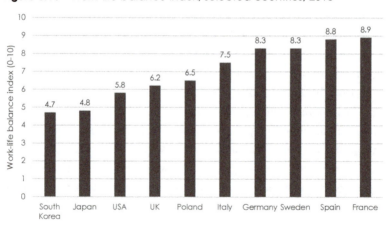

Source: OECD Better Life Index, 2018 or the latest available.

The remaining part of this section will examine why Japan's fertility rate remains relatively low despite government measures to promote the fertility rate. It will consider the aspects of money (financial capability) and time (temporal capability) available to (young) Japanese couples and three relevant factors will be investigated: the negative impact of labour market deregulation since the late 1990s on the fertility rate, government policy to promote the fertility rate such as daycare provision and maternity leave, and the change in social norms on marriage.

Labour market deregulation implemented by the LDP government since the late 1990s has had a negative impact on Japan's fertility rate by increasing the number of young low-paid non-regular workers. Against the background of economic stagnation since the collapse of the bubble economy and the intensified international competition from neighbouring Asian countries, Japanese employers have sought to reduce their labour costs and increase labour flexibility by increasing the use of non-regular workers, especially among young workers. As can be seen in Figure 5.1, the percentage of regular workers has declined among young workers and by 2015, the percentage of non-regular workers was slightly higher than the percentage of regular workers in the age group 15–24. The increase in low-paid non-regular workers among the young has reduced the capacity for young Japanese to get married and have a family. As seen in the previous section, the percentage of the working poor whose annual income is less than ¥2 million has increased since the implementation of labour market deregulation and reached between 16 and 25 per cent of the total work force. A high percentage of the working poor are young workers who cannot afford to have a family, and this has contributed to the country's low fertility rate.

Japan's fertility rate has remained low despite the government's attempt to increase the number of daycare centers. The problem was first recognized when the total fertility rate dropped to 1.57 in 1989 (the "1.57 shock"). Daycare services for children had not satisfied the needs of working mothers because there were many rigid regulations on, among other things, the operators, location and their business hours. The government had not issued licences to run daycare centers to private corporations, and those authorized daycare services provided were standardized. The strong presence of public-sector unions in the childcare industry further hindered the provision of flexible services (Boling 2007: 135; Wada 2007: 159). The public policy regarding daycare service caused inconvenience to working mothers who sought to balance jobs and child rearing and this inconvenience encouraged them to stay at home or engage only in part-time jobs.

However, after the "1.57 shock", the LDP government launched several programmes to deal with this problem in the 1990s. The first was the "Angel Plan" in December 1994, which sought to eliminate the economic and social obstacles to child rearing (Boling 1998; House of Councillors 1996). The Angel Plan instigated five-year emergency childcare projects from 1995 until 1999. These included the provision of daycare for 0–2-year old, extended daycare hours, and temporary and short-time daycare. The government also encouraged private companies to reduce working times and to establish in-house daycare centers. In addition, the government sought to improve housing conditions, reduce competition in education and increase education loans as well as introduce lower daycare service fees for dual-work families to help reduce the cost of raising children.

However, the success rate of many projects under the Angel Plan was not high, partly because local government, which undertook the projects assigned by the Ministry of Health and Welfare (MHW), lacked the human and financial resources. The MHW was forced to give up accomplishing the original goals set by the Angel Plan and lowered the targets by as much as 50 per cent in 1998. These unsatisfactory results, however, also owed much to the slow pace of deregulation in daycare services undertaken by the MHW. Many licenced daycare centers could not satisfy the needs of working mothers in terms of service hours and the age of children who can receive daycare, and unlicenced centers had to accommodate many children in excess of their capacities. In Tokyo, there were about 10,000 "waiting children" (*taiki jidō*), children on waiting lists for daycare centers, aged 0–2 years old in 1996.

In 1997, the LDP government amended the Child Welfare Law in order to facilitate the participation of private corporations in daycare business and consulting service for child rearing. In July 1999, the government provided ¥200 billion in temporary special subsidies to local governments as an extraordinary measure (applied only to projects to be initiated by the end of 1999) to address the problem of children waiting for admission to daycare centers (Kōseishō 1999a). Projects covered by the subsidies included the construction of daycare facilities near train stations (*ekimae hoikuen*), implementation of daycare services in kindergartens, short-time daycare for children after illness, the training of at-home daycare service providers, and daycare services in public facilities (Kōseishō 1999b).

After the unsuccessful implementation of the Angel Plan, the government devised the "New" Angel Plan in December 1999 with the participation of almost all ministries compared to the participation of only the four ministries of Health and Welfare, Labour, Education and Construction in the case of the previous plan. In the New Angel Plan, operative between 2000 and 2004, the solution to the problem of waiting children was again a priority, and the expansion of capacity of daycare centers was emphasized. A number of initiatives were established, including improved daycare for infants (0–2 year old), mid-year admission to daycare centers, extended-hours, weekend provision (experimental), emergency and temporary services for single parent families ("short-stay" and "twilight-stay" services), provision of childcare at home with the cooperation of the National Babysitters Association, and the establishment of family support centers run by the Ministry of Labour (Tochio 2000: 14–17).

Except in the provision of daycare centers, the Japanese government provided a low level of child welfare services and depended on families and businesses for the provision of those services. Compared with many other industrialized countries, Japan's level of child allowance (*jidō teate*) was low. When first introduced in 1971, the amount was only a few thousand yen per month and not available to the first two children. It was also means tested and was not available to those families beyond a certain income ceiling. In terms of the ratio of child allowance to total social welfare expenditure, Japan's was much lower than those of the Nordic countries (Osawa 1993: 199; Osawa 1996: 46–8). The Japanese government instead depended on companies for the provision of financial support for families with children in the form of family allowances (*kazoku teate*), which included an allowance for the spouse (*haigūsha teate*) and an allowance for the support of children and grandparents (*fuyō teate*). However, as already noted, if wives received an annual salary above ¥1.03 million, family allowances were not provided.

Although child allowance is a major tool of state financial support to families with children in many OECD countries, the role played by child allowance in Japan has been much less significant (Osawa 1993: 199). Child allowance was principally for low-income households in Japan, and child rearing allowance (*jidō fuyō teate*), which was higher than child allowance, was only available for single-mother families. Child allowance of ¥5,000 per month was paid for each of the first two children and for the third and later children ¥10,000 per month was paid. An income ceiling was set at ¥2,840,000 for a four-person household from June 1999. The expansion of child allowance was discussed as a measure to reduce economic burden on families with children before entering elementary schools and had been expected to be a solution to the problem of fewer children. The participation of Kōmeitō Party, which had demanded the expansion of child allowance, in the coalition government from October 1999 helped the reluctant LDP deal with this issue. As a result, special child allowance was paid to families with children who were three years or older and before their entrance to elementary school (and paid until the end of the year when the child became 6 years old). The amount of the allowance remained ¥5,000 per month for the first and second child and ¥10,000 yen for the third and later children, but the income ceiling was extended to ¥4,325,000 for self-employed families and ¥6,700,000 for employed families.

Maternity Leave Law became effective in April 1992. Originally applicable only to companies with 30 or more employees, it was extended to include companies with less than 30 employees after 1995. However, the law was not applicable to employees employed on a daily basis or for a fixed period. Financial support for working mothers related to maternity leave included the payment of maternity leave allowance and the exemption from social welfare payment during maternity leave. The amount of maternity leave allowance was 25 per cent of the salary (20 per cent was paid during the period of maternity leave as "maternity leave basic allowance" and the remaining 5 per cent was paid 6 months after the return to work as "maternity leave return-to-work allowance"). The amount of maternity leave allowance (for a period of 6 weeks prior to and 8 weeks after childbirth) and childcare leave allowance (for a period after maternity leave of up to one year with a possibility of a longer period in certain cases) was raised to 40 per cent of salary in January 2001 (and is currently 67 per cent). Furthermore, to promote the use of maternity leave by female employees, the government subsidized employers for the costs of hiring cover for the employee and implementing a return-to-work programme for maternity-leave takers.

Although government services for child rearing improved to some extent in the 1990s, the structural reforms implemented by the Koizumi administration between 2001 and 2006 that aimed to reduce the government deficit by cutting the government spending saw childcare services negatively affected, as the construction of public childcare centers slowed down while the privatization of childcare services was promoted (Boling 2007: 143–4). Together with the labour market deregulation, the working conditions of childcare providers also deteriorated, as some of them in regular status were replaced by those in non-regular status. However, recognizing these negative effects, the following LDP administrations between 2006 and 2009 enabled prefectural governments to increase the number of daycare centers with a newly established government fund, and the DPJ government between 2009 and 2012 increased the amount of child allowance by enabling all families with children to receive it irrespective of the amount of their annual income (Hagiwara, 2013). The DPJ government also continued the LDP policy of expanding childcare centers.

Although original "Abenomics" focused on the achievement of economic growth and did not refer to Japan's low fertility rate, its lack of success prompted the Abe administration to announce, as part of "new" Abenomics in September 2015, two ambitious social welfare objectives of increasing the fertility rate to 1.8 and eliminating job resignation due to the need to provide elderly care (*kaigo rishoku*). These measures for increasing the fertility rate were also aimed at promoting economic growth by increasing the construction of daycare facilities and the economic contribution of a female labour force. In addition, the Abe administration sensationally announced the "Human Resource Revolution" (*hitozukuri kakumei*) in 2017, which proposed the introduction of free childcare for all children between the ages of three and five irrespective of family income (in addition to free childcare for children aged between 0 and 2 for low-income families exempted from paying the residential tax).

However, recent government attempts to increase the fertility rate with new Abenomics and the Human Resource Revolution are problematic. Firstly, and most importantly, the Abe administration has not taken any serious measures to improve the working conditions of childcare providers. Secondly, the current situation of insufficient number of childcare providers will be further exacerbated with the increasing number of children now able to access free childcare. Working conditions of childcare providers remain poor in terms of both pay and quality of work despite the great demand for their services. Currently, the monthly income of childcare providers is about ¥100,000 lower than the average of those in all industrial sectors. As a result, childcare is not a popular job in Japan. So, despite an increasing number of childcare centers and the greater availability of free childcare, the problem of under capacity will not be easily solved until the poor working conditions of childcare providers is tackled.

In addition to the shortcomings in public policy, Japan's employment practices, which as we documented earlier in the chapter force men to work for long hours and discriminate against women, have also contributed to the country's low fertility rate (see also Boling 2007). While the recent changes in labour laws such as those to be implemented through the Work-Style Reform from 2019 may change these employment practices to some extent, they are unlikely to be fundamental and contribute to the improvement of the fertility rate to a significant extent. For example, although Japan's maternity leave became more generous recently with a higher amount of maternity pay and the percentage of Japanese women who utilize maternity leave has also increased (currently, female workers are entitled to receive 67 per cent of their salary for the first six months and 50 per cent for the following six months provided eligibility requirements are met such as the contribution to employment insurance), it has not contributed to a rise in the fertility rate to a significant extent. Many women still suffer from harassment when they request maternity leave (so-called "*matahara*", maternity harassment) and some women quit their jobs instead of utilizing maternity leave. There are pressures coming from employers, who want to contain labour costs, and from work colleagues, who want to avoid a greater workload if the employer does not provide replacement cover. *Matahara* has only made it more difficult for Japanese women to strike a good work–life balance and some have even given up having a child, which can only negatively affect the country's fertility rate.

Changes in social norms concerning marriage, especially among the younger generation, might also have affected Japan's fertility rate negatively. There is no longer the same pressure on younger people to get married. For some women, it is much more attractive to remain as a "parasite single" (*parasaito shinguru*) and to continue to comfortably live unmarried with their parents well into their late-20s and 30s (Yamada 2007: 109–17; 2009: 47–60). When Japanese women have a child, they can expect the "dual shift" of work at a company and childcare at home, with little help from their husbands who stay at work for long hours. By remaining as "parasite singles", they can continue working without any childcare duty, save money or buy expensive brand goods should they wish, as they have no rent to pay.

DECLINING POPULATION, REVITALIZATION OF
REGIONAL ECONOMIES AND LABOUR MIGRATION

In addition to an aging population and low fertility rates, Japan has experienced a decline in population, which has brought about the problem of labour shortage. While labour shortage has contributed to the improvement of working conditions of non-regular workers (e.g. wage hikes in economic sectors such as construction and elderly care), it has also contributed to the economic stagnation of rural and regional areas, such that rural revitalization has become an urgent policy issue, involving national and local government, politicians, private business, NGOs and local residents such as farmers. In 2009, the Ministry of Internal Affairs and Communication (MIC) initiated the programme "*chiiki okoshi kyōryoku-tai*" (regional revitalization cooperation army) to support urban to rural migration, which provided migrants with a local government job with an annual salary of about ¥2 million, but only with limited success. Indeed, most rural areas have not overcome the problems of population decline and economic stagnation (Asahi Shimbun 2019d). In the worst cases, some rural communities have simply vanished.

International migration to rural and regional areas has contributed to their revitalization to some extent by providing a workforce to industries in those areas, such as agriculture, food processing, construction and elderly care, which need labour input to maintain their economic activities. Against the background of regional economic integration in East Asia due to the expansion of regional supply chains, Japan entered into economic partnership agreements (EPAs) with the Philippines, Indonesia and Vietnam in 2006, 2007 and 2008 respectively, and received labour migrants from these countries in the elderly care sector. This sector, which is characterized by low-pay and poor working conditions, has suffered from severe labour shortage, whether in urban centers or rural areas. Labour migrants from these countries are expected to fill the gap between labour demand and supply in this sector to some extent, although the problem of low pay and poor working conditions remains. In addition, the xenophobic attitude of some Japanese people may also have contributed to the difficulty of migrant workers integrating in Japanese society and workplaces.

The Technical Intern Training Programme, which provides employment opportunities for foreign nationals, has also provided de facto labour migrants to help plug the gap between labour demand and supply. However, their working conditions remain very poor and precarious (Watanabe 2018b). This is partly because of the institutional arrangements of migration in their home countries (typically East Asian countries such as China, the Philippines and Vietnam) and the host country. The typical migration process includes finding a migrant recruiting agent or broker in the home country, borrowing money to pay the agent the pre-departure costs (obtaining a passport and an entry visa and so on) and a period of basic training to prepare for work in the host country. This process can take from 6 to 12 months. Brokers in Japan (*"kanri dantai"*, literally supervising organizations), which are monitored and supervised by quasi-government agencies, allocate technical interns to user companies or individual users such as farmers. With a weak regulations on the protection of technical interns and inadequate supervision of brokers and employers, many technical interns have suffered from severe abuse and exploitation by user companies and individual users, including the threat of dismissal and deporting, passport confiscation, and refusal to pay for work already done (Japan Times 2017). Technical interns also owe a large debt to an immigration agency or broker in their home country and are in effect forced to continue working to repay the debt despite poor working conditions.

One of the reasons for the continued poor working conditions of migrant workers, especially technical interns, is insufficient response to this situation by Japanese labour unions. As mentioned above, Japanese enterprise unions tend to ignore the plight of individual workers' working conditions. The case of migrant workers is even worse, as most of them are non-regular workers and enterprise unions have hardly any incentive to protect migrant workers by organizing them. Although national union confederations such as Rengō and some industrial federations talk about worker solidarity, migrant workers usually do not figure in their considerations.

The only unions that are concerned about the poor working conditions of migrant workers are individually-affiliated unions such as community unions and general unions. Among the most well-known are Zentōitsu Workers Union (All-United Workers Union) and the Kanagawa City Union (Kremers 2014; Urano & Stewart 2007; Watanabe 2018b). These unions often engage in social movement unionism by forming a coalition with social movement NGOs so that they can engage in the activities to improve the working conditions of migrant workers more effectively. In the case of Zentōitsu Workers Union, the union formed an institutional-ized coalition with the Solidarity Network with Migrants Japan (SMJ) and together have been politically active lobbying government bureaucrats (Kremers 2014; Watanabe 2018b). Individually-affiliated unions also have played a significant role in helping migrant workers by participating in dispute resolutions and providing legal advice and consultation. However, with their limited resources these unions have been unable to improve the working conditions of all migrant workers, and the solution to the poor working conditions of migrant workers needs worker solidarity involving enterprise unions. However, this is almost impossible, given the interests and incentives provided to enterprise unions. Although labour and immi-gration policy that provides migrant workers with better protection is essential to improve their working conditions, the Japanese government's response has not been enough, partly because it has been more concerned about the control of immigration to prevent (permanent) residency and citizenship than about the protection of migrant workers.

The Japanese government has maintained an official policy of non-immigration, or more precisely, no large-scale immigration of foreign-ers who intend to settle in Japan (see Roberts 2018 for the Japanese definition of immigration, or "*imin*" in Japanese). While welcoming immigration of highly-skilled workers by relaxing the conditions under which they can apply for permanent residency (although the number of these workers is much lower than the number of highly-skilled workers in English-speaking countries, for example), the Japanese government has maintained a policy of restricted immigration of low-skilled workers. However, to cope with the recent labour shortage in economic sectors such as agriculture, construction, retail and elderly care, Japanese employers have had to rely on the foreign labour force such as migrant workers (including those under EPAs), technical interns and foreign students, who are entitled to engage in part-time work while studying under certain conditions. The government has allowed, or has not imposed strict control of, the use of technical interns in the workplaces even when they may not provide the skill training officially expected to be provided to those technical interns.

The Japanese government enacted an amendment to the Immigration Control Law in 2016, partly in response to the criticisms about poor working conditions of technical interns (Roberts 2018: 98). However, the amendment was also aimed at expanding the scope of migrant workers for low-skilled jobs to cope with the labour shortages, which was more important from the government and employers' perspectives. For example, elderly care work was permitted for both the technical internship programme and foreign students' part-time work. Before the 2016 amendment, elderly care work could be provided only by those migrant workers who were authorized under Japan's EPA with the Philippines, Indonesia and Vietnam (Onuki 2009). The duration of stay as technical interns was also extended from three to five years (Roberts 2018: 98).

The enactment of the Technical Intern Law in 2016 (implemented in 2017) sought to ensure proper implementation of technical internship and increase their protection, and it established the Organization for Technical Intern Training (OTIT). The 2016 law also stipulated the protection of technical interns by prohibiting brokers (supervisors of technical internship – *jisshū kanrisha*) from forcing interns to engage in an internship program against their will by resorting to violence, intimidation and other measures, forcing interns into a contract that stipulates a penalty in case of breach of contract, or into a contract that enables brokers to administer their savings, by prohibiting brokers and employers from confiscating a passport, and by entitling interns to report violations by employers to ministers and by prohibiting employers from treating interns unfairly for that reason.

The 2016 Technical Intern Law also stipulates the penalties for violation by brokers and employers, ranging from imprisonment between 1 and 10 years, and fines between ¥200,000 and ¥3 million depending on the nature of the offence. Despite the enactment of the legislation, there have been many reports (a little more than 7,000 in 2017 and a further increase in 2018) of technical interns who have fled their workplace because of employers' abuse and poor working conditions. From interviews conducted with around 2,800 technical interns who fled their workplace conducted by the Ministry of Justice in 2017, we know that the monthly salaries of many were less than ¥100,000 despite the fact that they needed to pay more than ¥1 million to brokers in their home countries (Asahi Shimbun 2018c).

The Immigration Control Law was further amended in December 2018, and implemented in April 2019, officially accepting low-skilled workers in some industrial sectors that suffer from labour shortage (as well as low labour productivity) such as agriculture, construction and elderly care (Asahi Shimbun 2018a). Labour shortage in these sectors has been severe and the Abe administration has faced strong demands from the employers in these sectors to reform the country's immigration control system so that they would be able to use a larger number of migrant workers. As discussed in Chapter 2, the administration has introduced a new immigration visa category called "designated" or "specified" skills (*tokutei ginō*), which are further divided into two categories. In the first category, those migrant workers who have "certain" work skills and Japanese language proficiency are allowed to live in Japan for five years maximum, although they are not allowed to bring their family members with them. This category is also aimed at technical interns who have resided in Japan for at least three years, enabling them to acquire a visa without taking a language exam. The government predicts many technical interns will change their immigration status to this visa category (Asahi Shimbun 2018d) and in this way, the government can also address criticism of the working conditions and human rights violation of technical interns. The second category of the designated skill visa is aimed at more experienced or "mature" workers who are judged to have higher skills. Those who apply for a visa in this category need to take both skills and language exams, and once passing, they are allowed to bring in family members and are able to renew a visa so that they may eventually qualify for permanent residency.

The 2018 amendment to the Immigration Control Law stipulates that employers should ensure proper working conditions such as the payment of salaries equivalent to those for Japanese workers, for the workers in both categories of designated skill visa. Workers in both categories are also entitled to change their jobs as long as they are in the same industrial sectors. The government estimates a maximum of 350,000 migrant workers will work in the visa category of designated skills. However, to respond to criticism from those Japanese who are against the expansion of low-skilled migration, the government can suspend it in those industrial sectors that are judged no longer to suffer from labour shortage.

Critics of the 2018 amendment have questioned what limits exist on the scope for expanding the industrial sectors where migrant workers in the designated skills visa can be employed. With the 2018 amendment, employers in only 14 industrial sectors (agriculture, fishery, construction, elderly care, restaurants, hotels, building cleaning, food processing, material industry, industrial machinery, electronics and electrical equipment, shipbuilding, automobile maintenance and airline industry) are permitted to employ migrant workers in the visa category of designated skills. However, some business sectors, such as convenience stores, are already showing interest in recruiting those migrant workers (Asahi Shimbun 2018b). Critics also argue that it is not clear how the government will define the "certain" and "mature" skills relevant to the first and second visa categories of designated skills respectively. Critics have also claimed that hardly any discussion has been made on how to support and integrate those migrant workers into Japanese society, whereas the government has been more concerned about how to control them. Other criticisms voiced have been that the provision of social welfare services to these migrant workers and the payment of social insurance premiums has been insufficiently discussed, along with concern over increased crime, a downward pressure on the wages of Japanese workers, and the absence of measures to prevent technical interns from moving to and concentrating in large cities. While the Japanese government aims to transform Japan into an attractive country for migrant workers, critics claim that the condition for the first visa category that they cannot bring in family members is a violation of human rights, and this restrictive condition could deter some migrant workers from applying for the first visa category. Also, given the government's official position of no (large-sale, permanent) immigration and the criticism from conservative politicians that the creation of the second visa category may result in large-sale immigration based on permanent residency, the criteria for the second visa category might have been set too high for migrant workers to apply (Asahi Shimbun 2018b).

Many of these criticisms are justified, and in particular there is hardly any way to prevent those current technical interns who work in rural areas from moving to large cities with higher minimum wages once they obtain a new visa of designated work skills. This is likely to exacerbate the already poor economic situations in many rural and regional areas suffering from declining population and labour shortage. Unlike the technical internship programme, which prohibits technical interns from moving to another area for a new job or training programme, foreign workers in the designated skills visa are allowed to change jobs and move to a new area as long as they are in the same industrial sector.

Despite opposition from conservative supporters, the current Abe administration has decided to officially accept low-skilled migrant workers in response to the demands from employers who need them to cope with labour shortages. As the main reason for this decision by Prime Minister Abe was to address the concerns of his business supporters and to win election to the House of Councillors in 2019, it is expected that the poor working conditions of migrant workers will not be sufficiently addressed and their protection will remain the government's secondary concern at best. Prime Minister Abe regards labour shortages as a factor to hinder economic growth, which he needs to rectify to remain in power.

6

A distinctive Japanese economic feature: "Galapagos" syndrome

This chapter will critically examine the distinctive features of the Japanese economy, in particular what has been termed the "Galapagos" syndrome, and the reasons for it, which include the legacy of the "developmental state" and the outcome of interest group politics. The chapter will identify, among other things, anti-competitive business practices within industries and government regulations that protect Japanese companies from foreign rivals and deter competition at the cost of consumers. The chapter aims to identify the myths and realities of the Japanese economy.

"GALAPAGOS" SYNDROME: JAPAN'S FAILURE TO MEET THE GLOBAL STANDARD

In Japan, there are some unusual, often inefficient, business practices and services that do not meet the global standard. Together these practices have been termed "Galapagos" syndrome, as an analogy to the Galapagos Islands which underwent its own evolutionary changes in isolation from the mainland. The term was first used to refer to "non-smart" Japanese mobile phones, which were widely adopted in Japan, but unsuccessful elsewhere. These phones are called "*Garakei*", or *Galapagos keitai* (*keitai* is the Japanese word for a mobile phone) and before smart phones appeared, they were a technologically advanced product, which allowed people to use the Internet, send email and watch TV programmes. Even after smart phones first appeared in Japan, 40 per cent of mobile phone users in Japan still use Garakei and Japanese mobile phone service providers continue to offer Garakei services. In the case of Japan's largest mobile phone service provider NTT "Docomo" ("Do Communication by Mobile", a typical example of "Engrish"), which has a larger number of older users compared to the other two major providers (KDDI au and Softbank), around 50 per cent use Garakei. Japanese mobile phone service providers also offer newer "Garaho" (Galapagos smart phones), which are Garakei-type flip handsets that can use smartphone apps like social networking services. All three major mobile phone service providers offer Garaho plans and Japanese companies (Sharp, Fujitsu, Kyocera, NEC and Panasonic) manufacture them. Instead of disappearing, Japanese Garakei, and the more advanced Garaho, continue to exist and develop in their own Japanese way.

Garakei feature phones are a good example of a Japanese technology that has pursued a very different path to global mobile phone developments. Japanese banking services are another example of the Galapagos syndrome. The majority of ATMs in Japan do not accept bank cards issued outside of Japan with a few exceptions such as those in 7-Eleven convenience stores and post offices. Business hours of most Japanese banks in retail services dealing with individual customers are only from 9am to 3pm, Monday through Friday (although there have been some improvements recently) and ATM users are charged extra fees to withdraw cash in the evening and on weekends. Japan remains a cash society, so this inconvenience is even more costly for Japanese people. In 2018, the percentage of people using non-cash payments such as debit/credit cards and mobile phone payments was only 18.4 per cent (Nihon Keizai Shimbun 2018c). Japanese contactless, rechargeable payment cards like those used on public transport systems (e.g. Pasmo, Suica, etc.), typically need to be topped-up in cash, so even Japan's e-money system is not a completely non-cash method of payment. Other Galapagos features include Japanese banks still providing a paper "passbook" for their customers to check their record of transactions. Although online bank statements are available in Japan, many people still prefer to use a passbook.

The use of debit cards has also been limited in Japan. At first, major Japanese banks such as former Mitsubishi Bank, Mitsui Bank and Sumitomo Bank created their own "J-Debit" system, which was different from global brands such as Visa and Mastercard. J-Debit was hardly used, partly because many retail shops did not have a card reader to accept J-Debit cards, and even now, there is hardly any supermarket or convenience store that accepts J-Debit. Having given up with J-Debit, Japanese banks have begun to issue debit cards with Visa and Mastercard (also JCB, Japan Credit Bureau, which is a Japanese credit company but is little known outside Japan), so the use of debit cards has been increasing gradually. Sony Bank, the banking business subsidiary of Sony Corporation, issues its own brand of Visa debit card called "Sony Bank Wallet", which boasts that the users of Wallet can withdraw foreign currencies abroad (see the website of Sony Bank) – a routine and long-established practice outside Japan. However, even the users of Sony Bank Wallet still need to exchange in advance Japanese yen into the foreign currency they would like to withdraw abroad, so it is not convenient at all. Although Sony Bank Wallet may be slightly better or more advanced than other Japanese bank cash cards, which cannot be used to withdraw money outside Japan, it remains a Galapagos phenomenon. In addition, "contactless" debit or credit cards were unheard of in Japan until 2018 and even now the use of contactless cards is extremely limited. Similarly, integrated circuit (IC) chips for debit and credit cards were introduced only recently. As of 2018, only 17 per cent of Japanese debit/credit cards have IC chips, whereas in the US, the percentage is 47 per cent, and in Europe it is 99 per cent. Not surprisingly, the lack of debit/credit cards with IC chips has made Japan a good target for fake or counterfeit cards (Asahi Shimbun 2018e). The Japanese government and credit card companies aim to introduce IC chips to all credit cards by 2020, when Tokyo planned to hold the Olympics, to prevent illegal use of credit cards (Nihon Keizai Shimbun 2015). However, progress has been slow.

Similarly, Japanese consumers have not been able to use the normal online taxi-booking services or ride-sharing services that are widely available outside Japan. Uber has been prevented from setting up its own fleet of drivers in Japan as regulations prevent owners of private cars from transporting paying customers and has been forced to partner with existing taxi companies. As a result, customers do not get the benefit of flexible taxi fares based on Uber's cutting-edge algorithm (Nihon Keizai Shimbun 2018a). The only thing Uber has been able to do in Japan since launching there in 2015 is operate under its premium chauffeur brand, Uber Black, which are more expensive than normal Japanese taxies by 20–50 per cent. Most users of Uber Japan are foreign tourists and they pay more only for the convenience of booking a taxi online (in English) and being able to use a debit/credit card already set up in their Uber account. Son Masayoshi, CEO of Softbank, one of the three major mobile phone service providers in Japan, complained "Ride-sharing is prohibited by law in Japan. I can't believe there is still such a stupid country" (Reuters 2018). Softbank has invested in several online taxi booking or ride-sharing companies around the world and attempted to expand this business in Japan, but government regulation has prevented it from doing so (Nihon Keizai Shimbun 2018b).

Other random examples of "Galapagos Japan" include a lack of self-order kiosks and self-service checkouts in supermarkets, convenience stores and fast-food chains, which are common features of convenience shopping in other countries; expensive international phone calls, which are much higher than those in many other countries; and prohibitively expensive overseas travel insurance sold by Japanese insurance companies compared to equivalent policies from overseas companies.

One Galapagos phenomenon worth highlighting is in the area of broadcasting and communications. Japanese broadcasters do not provide simultaneous broadcasting on terrestrial television and Internet, with only a few exceptions (e.g. emergency disaster information). NHK (Nihon Hōsō Kyōkai, Japan Broadcasting Corporation), which is a Japanese national public corporation administered by the Ministry of Internal Affairs and Communications (MIC), has requested permission to provide simultaneous terrestrial and Internet broadcasting services to prepare for

2020 Tokyo Olympics. However, private broadcasting corporations have complained that this would give NHK disproportionate market control as it would be costly for them to provide similar services. The expert committee of the MIC decided to approve the NHK plan only if NHK satisfies certain conditions such as its sharing its infrastructure for simultaneous broadcasting with private corporations (Asahi Shimbun 2018f). It is difficult to understand the objections of private broadcasting corporations in Japan when simultaneous services are provided by private broadcasting corporations in other countries throughout the world. The complaint is a typical response from vested interest seeking to protect their business, and a characteristic tactic of Japanese big business. The interests of the general public in receiving services deemed unexceptional and routine in other countries are undermined as a result.

A LACK OF DIGITALIZATION AND ECONOMIC INEFFICIENCY

While the Japanese economy has been competitive and efficient in manufacturing sectors such as automobiles and electronics (although electronics less than it was), other sectors, particularly finance, insurance and telecommunications, have suffered from economic inefficiency and low labour productivity (see Figure 3.4 for international comparisons of productivity). One of the chief reasons for this has been the lack of digitalization in the Japanese economy.

As already mentioned, the use of debit cards (and credit cards and smartphone payment) is not popular in Japan, although their use is increasing, especially since the increase in consumption tax from 8 to 10 per cent in October 2019 and government measures to rebate those customers that used cashless payment. Instead, most transactions are conducted by cash payment and Japan remains a cash society. According to the 2018 data of Japan's Ministry of Economy, Trade and Industry (METI), the percentage of consumers who made cashless payments for the purchase of goods and services in Japan is among the lowest in selected countries (see Figure 6.3). And as mentioned above, the Japanese percentage also includes smart

cards, which often need top-up by cash. To use online top-up, users usually need to apply by sending an application in writing! Although smartphone payment is becoming more popular in Japan, the percentage of
those aged 20–69 who used smartphone payment was only 9 per cent in
March 2019 (Asahi Shimbun 2019e). One reason for the low use may be
that users need to create a payment account linked to a bank account and
transfer money from the bank account to the payment account in advance
as users of smartcards need to do. Coupled with the ID checks that need
to be gone through online, it is no surprise that these cumbersome procedures mitigate against the use of smartphone payment. Indeed, 7pay, a
mobile payment app offered by 7-Eleven Japan, was forced to suspend its
service within a few days of launching because hackers exploited a flaw
in the online procedures (Asahi Shimbun 2019f).

Figure 6.1 Cashless payments (percentage of total payments),
selected countries, 2015

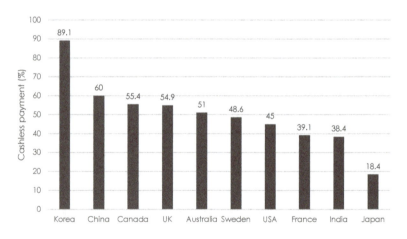

Source: Ministry of Economy, Trade and Industry, *Cashless Vision*, 2018.

Asked why Japanese shops and restaurants do not accept debit or
credit cards, the reason most often cited (42%) was high fees due to the
credit card companies, according to METI survey in 2016 (Nihon Keizai

Shimbun 2018d). The government has recently requested credit card companies to lower the fee they impose on small retail shops to make it easier and more affordable for these shops to introduce debit or credit card payment (METI aims to increase the cashless transaction rate from the current 18 per cent to 40 per cent by 2025). Japanese banks provide very poor and inefficient services in terms of online banking, but they have plans to introduce mobile phone payments at convenience stores and debit services using smart phones reading QR codes at retail shops (Nihon Keizai Shimbun 2018c). It remains to be seen, however, if and to what extent Japanese banks will be able to provide better online banking services. Getting rid of their reliance on paper application documents is a necessary first step, otherwise their services will remain poor and inefficient.

The prevalence of paper-based transactions and a lack of online transactions are not limited to banking transactions, however. Most of the administrative services provided by national and local governments to Japanese citizens and foreign tourists are still paper-based and not digitalized. Online processes for administrative services hardly exist and Japanese citizens still need to go to a local city or town office to obtain official documents such as a civil registration document (*koseki*) or residential certificate (*jūminhyō*) issued by the local government. What can be done online is limited to downloading application forms for official documents that then need to be completed with black ball-point pen, before attaching a seal (*hankō*) and bringing it to a city or town office or posting it. There are no e-visa services for foreign visitors yet, although there are plans to start one for Chinese tourists in April 2020 (Nihon Keizai Shimbun 2018e). Despite Prime Minister Abe's wish to promote e-government, indeed his intention to transform Japan into among the most advanced IT nations, the online services provided by national and local governments remain extremely underdeveloped and far behind many countries (Nihon Keizai Shimbun 2013c).

The lack of online transactions in government administrative services and the problems this causes has repeatedly been seen in the extremely poor services provided by the Japan Pension Service (JPS, previously the Social Insurance Agency). Instead of asking pensioners to submit necessary information online, the JPS has asked them to provide information on a paper document and then manually keyed that data into their computer database. However, this has resulted in repeated errors in the inputting of data by the JPS, and in some cases records of pensioners have been deleted. As a result, pensioners who had paid premiums have received a much smaller amount of pension or no pension at all despite their complaints. These fiascos have become political issues. For example, as is well known, the massive disappearance of pension records and the receipt of much smaller pensions by those pensioners affected contributed to the LDP loss in the election to the House of Councillors in 2007 and the demise of the first Abe administration.

The obvious question to be asked is why hadn't the JPS introduced an online system for the data input and asked pensioners to fill out an online form instead of a paper form? The fiasco could have been avoided if the JPS dealt with the data digitally and eliminated the completely unnecessary process of manual input. However, despite repeated mishandling of pensioners' data, most recently in February 2018, the JPS has yet to introduce an online system for data input. Instead, the JPS has announced that it would seek a better way for data input by paper transaction (Asahi Shimbun 2018g). The JPS has introduced a basic online service called "*Nenkin Netto*" (Pension Internet Service) so that users of the service are able to check their pension record. However, it too suffers from non-standard inefficiencies and inconveniences that other systems seek to avoid. For example, those who wish to use the service cannot choose their user ID or password, and they cannot complete the registration process online either, as the JPS needs to confirm the identity of applicants for an account and send a user ID by post. And an application number, which needs to be retained for future use, needs to be written down as no email including this number is sent to applicants.

Perhaps one of the stranger oddities of Galapagos Japan is the continuing use of fax (facsimile) machines – the telephonic transmission of scanned printed material, typically to a telephone number connected to a printer. According to a survey conducted by the Ministry of Internal Affairs and Communications (MIC) in 2006, 97.8 per cent of Japanese companies used fax. Also, 42 per cent of Japanese households used fax according to a MIC survey conducted in 2015. While a fax machine is exhibited as a historical object in the Smithsonian Museum in Washington, DC, many Japanese companies and business owners as well as households still use fax machines for business and personal transactions instead of using a PDF attachment to an email. Although the sale of fax machines decreased from around 11 million in 2005 to around 2.86 million in 2010, the sales figure has remained constant since then and about 2 million fax machines were sold in 2015.

Various reasons have been given for the continued use of such an outdated product (by international standards) such as its popularity with a large number of elderly owners of small shops who do not understand how to use Internet or email, the path-dependent, conservative nature of Japanese business practices, and the continued existence of business customers that continue to use fax. It is a popular topic for discussion on websites forums and blogs in Japan and fax has both supporters and detractors. Those who have positive views cite that those who are not computer literate can still use fax machines, that they need to use fax machines because of the Japanese custom to attach a seal (*hankō*) for business approval, that handwriting on fax paper could be quicker and more efficient than typing Japanese words using a computer as frequent conversions between *hiragana* (Japanese characters) and *kanji* (Chinese characters) are necessary to write Japanese sentences, and so on. Those who criticize the use of fax machines cite them as detrimental to raising the efficiency and productivity of Japanese business, and that their use is costly as they need to pay for phone calls, paper and ink toner.

It was widely reported in early 2019 when the new Chairman of Japan's largest business organization, Keidanren (Japanese Business Federation), also the Chairman of Hitachi Corporation, made the remark that he was surprised not to find a computer in the office of the Keidanren Chairman, which prompted social media speculation that "the previous Chairmen of Keidanren did not or could not use Internet" and it was "a symbol of Japan as an IT laggard" (Asahi Shimbun 2018h). Overseas news media also reported in late 2018 that the new Cybersecurity Minister of Japan had admitted not ever having used a computer and apparently did not know what a USB memory stick was (Asahi Shimbun 2018i). According to the World Competitiveness Rankings published by the International Institute of Business Management, Lausanne in 2019, out of 63 countries surveyed, Japan ranked 63rd in data usage capacity and 60th in data skill level (and 63rd in international experience of business executives and 62nd in language ability). Japan's overall ranking, which included other areas of competitiveness, was 30th (Nihon Keizai Shimbun 2019a).

It is not only Japanese business, however, that does not use online services as much as their foreign counterparts. Japanese universities require paper applications unlike almost all universities outside Japan. Although applications by foreign students for exchange programmes have improved with some Japanese universities providing online application procedures, many still require paper application. The lack of digitalization in Japanese academia is also reflected in the low take-up of digital academic content, including e-books and e-journals, which in combination with the difficulty of understanding the Japanese language for most foreigners, has lessened the impact of Japanese academia outside Japan significantly.

The perception exists that Japan is a hi-tech country with a high Internet penetration and advanced mobile usage, but the reality is very different. Free public Wi-Fi is also far more limited in Japan than in other developed countries, although the situation has been gradually improving. Free public Wi-Fi is available only in a small number of cafes and restaurants in Japan. Starbucks, an American company, only began to provide this service as late as July 2012 and McDonalds only recently in 2018. Very few train companies, including *Shinkansen*, where tickets are very expensive, provide free Wi-Fi, especially on the train, although the situation has been improving partly due to the impending Tokyo Olympics in 2020. One of the reasons for a lack of free public Wi-Fi in Japan may be that people to date have done most things Net-related from their mobile phones and for these users, there was little demand for a network of free public Wi-Fi. It has been aimed at foreign tourists in Japan rather than Japanese people, and many train companies provide their free Wi-Fi services only to foreign tourists after they show their passports.

THE LEGACY OF THE "DEVELOPMENTAL STATE" AND INTEREST GROUP POLITICS

As we saw in Chapter 4, the Japanese developmental state pursued economic growth as its number one priority, and it intervened in the economy to promote economic activities in promising strategic sectors by implementing a pro-competitive industrial policy. However, the Japanese developmental state also implemented anti-competitive industrial policy aimed at protecting infant businesses and inefficient sectors from foreign competition. The "convoy" system that existed in financial sectors was a good example. The anti-competitive industrial policy also worked as a kind of social or employment policy to maintain jobs in inefficient sectors (Kume 2000). As a result, several outdated business practices and inefficient economic sectors have remained, and some products that have vanished from foreign markets still exist in Japan, such as computers made by the Japanese corporations of NEC, Fujitsu, Panasonic, etc., which are no longer sold outside Japan but are widely available in the Japanese market despite typically costing more than twice as much as comparable computers sold outside Japan. As shown in connection with Japanese travel insurance products, lack of competition from foreign companies and little change in products and services in the domestic market have enabled some Japanese companies to charge very high prices to consumers. Price differences between Japan and abroad was once one of the main issues of Japanese political economy, including the subject of trade disputes with the US, before the collapse of the bubble economy in the early 1990s. However, partly due to the relative decline of the Japanese economy since then, this does not gain the attention it once did (and now that China is the main target of the US in its trade disputes). Nevertheless, the need for Japanese consumers to be better served by Japanese business remains an important issue.

Anti-competitive self-regulation in private business sectors and interest group politics have also contributed to the survival of inefficient economic sectors, the lack of digitalization and the continued existence of Galapagos phenomena. Some business sectors have sought to protect themselves from competition from more efficient and competitive foreign companies with the use of non-tariff barriers (NTBs) against foreign companies that have attempted to enter the Japanese market.

The self-regulations have also deterred the merger and acquisition of Japanese companies by foreign companies and contributed to a lack of inward FDI in Japan. The percentage of inward FDI in Japan has remained at a very low level even since the Asian financial crisis in the late 1990s, when some Japanese banks and insurance companies were acquired by foreign companies, especially American companies (see Figure 4.3 for inward FDI per cent of GDP in Japan and selected countries). Even today, there are some economic sectors where foreign products are hardly seen, partly because of the self-regulations that have deterred foreign companies from investing (Mason 1999: 363–4). A lack of inward FDI can further impact by preventing the transfer of new technologies and business know-how from foreign companies. In addition, peculiar *keiretsu* activities such as cross-shareholding among *keiretsu* companies have also made it difficult for foreign companies to acquire Japanese companies.

Interest group politics has also contributed to inefficiency and Galapagos phenomena. To protect their vested interests, inefficient private business sectors have depended on the political support from the governing LDP, which has been dominant in Japanese politics since 1955 (except for about four years), and the LDP received votes and political donations in return (Pempel 2012). In this way, the mutual dependence between inefficient private business sectors and the LDP has been maintained at the cost of consumers. This also reflects Japan's quintessential corporate-centered society. Protection from foreign competition has enabled some

Japanese business sectors to remain inefficient and refrain from engaging in digitalization to enhance productivity and efficiency.

While bureaucrats are likely to have played a significant role in Japan's achievement of high economic growth in the 1960s, LDP *zoku* politicians since the beginning of Japan's lower economic growth in the 1970s have become more deeply engaged in particular economic sectors such that they have been able to offer policies that protect inefficient companies and provide them with subsidies in return for votes and political donations. As a result, these companies and individuals have lost any incentive or need to become more productive by, for example, promoting the efficiency of their business through digitalization, and continue to engage in business practices that do not satisfy the global standard.

Self-regulations in private business sectors made possible by lax implementation of anti-monopoly legislation by the LDP government may also have acted as a kind of social and employment policy aimed at maintaining jobs, in a similar manner to the government's industrial policy. For example, one of the reasons for the popularity and wide availability of CDs and DVDs in Japan (instead of download and streaming services) may be the protection of jobs in related economic industries. With digitalization and streaming services comes reduced production of CDs and DVDs and potential job losses for those engaged in such products. To maintain their employment, the relevant economic sectors may introduce self-regulations such as a cartel or other NTBs and the government of the LDP, whose *zoku* politicians protect inefficient economic sectors for electoral gain, is likely to allow the existence of such anti-competitive measures, which would be banned under competition legislation in many other countries. It could be argued that Japanese companies' continued use of the fax machine also works as an NTB for foreign companies that do not use fax machines!

Although perhaps not directly related to the Japanese economy, the recent controversy over whether an indoor smoking ban should be introduced ahead of the 2020 Tokyo Olympics is a good example of interest group politics at work. More than 50 countries, including the recent host cities of the Olympics, have banned indoor smoking in public places such as restaurants and bars (Japan Times 2018). However, LDP *zoku* politicians, who were backed by interest groups such as Japan Tobacco (JT) and restaurant and hospitality industries, opposed the initial proposal from the Ministry of Health, Labour and Welfare (MHLW) that sought a ban on smoking in eateries with a floor space of more than 30 square metres (restaurant and bar industries have opposed a smoking ban despite the fact that less than 20 per cent of Japanese people are smokers). After the anti-smoking MHLW Minister Shiozaki was replaced with the more tolerant Minister Kato, the MHLW compromised with the LDP *zoku* politicians and proposed a smoking ban only in eateries with a floor space of more than 100 square metres, which would allow smoking in more than 50 per cent of eateries. This was enacted into law in July 2018 as an amendment to the Law on the Promotion of Health (*Kenkō Zōshin Hō*) and will be implemented from April 2020 (Asahi Shimbun 2018j) (although Tokyo has passed a stricter anti-smoking ordinance similar to the original MHLW proposal). It is a good example of Japanese interest group politics in operation and which have contributed to the maintenance of practices that do not meet the global standard (or the standard of many industrialized countries in this case). In contrast, "outdoor" smoking on the streets is strictly banned in many Japanese cities for safety reasons except in designated smoking areas, which is yet another peculiar aspect of Japan's anti-smoking policy.

There are many other daily frustrations of a Galapagos nature that could be listed, from the disposal of household rubbish, which can only be done through local neighbourhood associations to which residents must be members (Asahi Shimbun 2018k), rather than being able to leave rubbish for collection outside residents' houses, to the obligation imposed on the executive members of Parents and Teachers Associations (PTA) to collect school lunch fees by visiting each student's house (Asahi Shimbun 2018l).

Despite the Japanese government's declaration in 2013 "to create a top leading IT nation in the world" (*sekai saisentan IT kokka sōzō sengen*) and to achieve this objective by 2020, the current situation is very far from achieving this (Nihon Keizai Shimbun 2013b, 2013c). Prime Minister Abe's own admission that he himself felt "nervous" when he used e-money and QR code "for the first time" in February 2019 shows a prime minister ambitious to transform Japan into the world's number one country in information technology is very unfamiliar with it (Asahi Shimbun 2019b). Similarly, his statement (and LDP official policy) of "Japan will create the No.1 business environment for foreign companies to do business" is also a far cry from the reality. There remain several government and private-sector regulations aimed at preventing the entry of foreign companies into the Japanese market. While Prime Minister Abe has sought to maintain the liberal international order in international trade, not necessarily for the sake of it but because it has benefitted Japan, he should also recognize the existence of non-tariff barriers in the Japanese market and the need to get rid of them. Also, he must address the corporate-centered nature of Japanese society which has paid little attention to the needs of consumers (or which only mention consumer benefits as "*tatemae*", "official lip service") due to the maintenance of vested interest by protective anti-competitive government and private-sector regulations. Instead of trumpeting Japan's greatness in empty and meaningless rhetoric, Prime Minister Abe would be better focused on ensuring the country overcomes its backward business practices by getting rid of paper transactions and promoting digitalization, and should recognize that Japan must first catch up with global standards before it can reassert its position in the global economy.

Conclusion: prospects and challenges for the Japanese economy

This book began with a historical analysis of the Japanese economy in the modern period (from the Meiji Restoration until the end of the Second World War), followed by an analysis of some major characteristics of the Japanese political economy from the end of the war until the bubble economy in the late 1980s. The collapse of the bubble economy in the early 1990s was a major turning point in the Japanese economy, and Chapter 2 examined the economic changes, as well as continuities, since then until the current period. Chapter 3 examined key indicators of the Japanese economy, including GDP, prices, the foreign sector (trade and FDI), the government sector (government expenditures and revenues, taxes and government deficits and debts) and the welfare state (pensions, health care, elderly care, including the socio-economic phenomena related to the welfare state such as inequality and poverty). Chapter 4 examined the structure of the Japanese economy in terms of state-market relations exemplified by the developmental state, institutional complementarities, convergence and diversity of capitalisms under globalization, the dual economy, and the impact of regional economic integration.

Chapter 5 focused on the human and labour factors of the Japanese economy. It examined the main characteristics of Japanese human resource management and industrial relations, including their changes and continuities, gender discrimination, and labour market dualism and diversification. The chapter also examined the negative impact of labour market reform on society in terms of the deterioration of working conditions and union response to this situation as well as low fertility rates. The chapter concluded by examining declining population, rural revitalization and labour migration, both domestic and international, as a solution to revitalize the rural and regional economies. In this respect, the chapter also discussed the problems related to international labour migration, especially the poor working conditions of migrant workers and the inadequate union response. Finally, Chapter 6 identified some phenomena that characterize Japan's "Galapagos" syndrome, its failure to meet the global standard. It then examined the lack of digitalization in Japan as a particular example of economic inefficiency and some of the reasons behind this, chief among them being the legacy of the developmental state and interest group politics. The chapter claimed that these political factors lay behind the government and private-sector business regulations that protect inefficient economic sectors and maintain business practices that do not meet the global standard.

In addition to the challenge of enhancing economic efficiency and raising labour productivity by promoting digitalization and meeting global standards, as discussed in Chapter 6, there are several challenges the Japanese economy will need to overcome in the future, which have been examined in previous chapters. These include: 1) low fertility rate and an aging population, 2) an increase in the working poor, 3) labour shortages, 4) the need to sustain social welfare provision despite huge levels of public debt, and 5) the continuing rise of China and regional economic integration in East Asia and the Asia Pacific

Japan's low fertility rate is likely to have a negative impact on economic growth due to a smaller amount of labour input. Along with an aging population and an increasing number of elderly people who rely on state pensions for sustaining their livelihood, the low fertility rate will make it more difficult for the government to maintain the public pension system and other social welfare services due to a smaller amount of government tax revenues. In order to increase the fertility rate, the government needs to implement policies that would make it more affordable for young couples to raise children and enable them to strike a better work-life balance. While the government, most recently the Abe administration, has proposed and implemented several policy measures aimed at increasing the number of day-care centers and increasing the amount of maternity pay and so on, these have not succeeded in increasing the fertility rate to any significant extent. The issue of "waiting children" remains a social problem in large cities despite an increase in the number of day-care centers administered by local governments. This is only likely to become more serious with the expected increase in applications for daycare places arising from the introduction of free day-care provision for children aged 3–5. The Japanese government needs to raise the working conditions of day-care providers in order to facilitate an increasing number of day-care providers.

The implementation of labour market deregulation since the 1990s, especially deregulation of non-regular employment, has contributed to a significant increase in the number of non-regular workers, such that currently, almost 40 per cent of workers in Japan are non-regular workers, as we have seen in Chapter 5. The low unemployment rates have arisen chiefly from labour shortage and not from Abenomics. In addition, most increase in employment has occurred in non-regular employment. What is problematic for the Japanese economy is that, as most non-regular workers are poorly paid, the number of "working poor" has increased. An increase in the working poor among young workers has also contributed to the low fertility rate, as it is more difficult to raise children with a small amount of salary. In addition, an increasing number of the working poor has negatively affected economic growth in Japan because of their lack of spending power. The government needs to enhance the protection of non-regular workers (and regular workers in SMEs) by improving the social safety net provisions, such as more generous unemployment insurance and the creation of the so-called "second safety net" between unemployment insurance and social (public) assistance as the last resort.

In order to overcome the challenge of labour shortage, the government has implemented policy measures to promote women's labour market participation. In addition to the policy measures already discussed in previous chapters, the current Abe administration has enacted the Women Activation Law (*Josei Katsuyaku Hō*), which obliges large companies to set targets for utilizing female labour to a greater extent. However, due to employer opposition, the Abe administration has had to compromise and as a result, companies can set targets without government scrutiny and assessment, or penalty. In addition, despite Prime Minister Abe's rhetoric of a labour market that is kind to working women, the administration has failed to significantly reform the tax system that favours families with full-time housewives and part-time working mothers in low income. This has highlighted a lack of serious intention of the Abe administration to promote women's labour market participation. After all, for the Abe administration, better working conditions for women is not simply a matter of equality but is for the sake of economic growth through their greater spending power.

Where a significant increase in the number of female workers cannot be expected, the government can only rely on labour migration (in addition to a greater usage of robotics and artificial intelligence). Despite the LDP's conservative attitude towards immigration, the current Abe administration has recently introduced new official routes for the immigration of low-skilled workers, albeit to a limited extent, by enacting the 2018 amendment to the Immigration Control Law. However, as mentioned in Chapter 5, the category 1 of the new visa is not attractive to labour migrants, as they are prevented from bringing with them family members and the immigration criteria for category 2 is equally strict. For these reasons, it is not clear if Japan will be able to compete with other countries in East Asia such as South Korea and Taiwan to attract the low-skilled workers needed to fill the labour shortage in sectors like elderly care, agriculture and construction. In this respect, the Abe administration's conservative and half-hearted attitude towards labour migration is problematic.

In 2018, Japan's public debt (both central and local governments) amounted to more than 250 per cent of the GDP, which is the highest level of public debt of the industrialized countries. The Abe administration's increase in fiscal spending and its postponement (twice) of a rise in consumption tax (only finally realized in October 2019) means a smaller budget at a time when it will need to cope with ever-increasing social welfare spending as a smaller number of the working population will have to finance a greater amount of social welfare spending for an aging population. It will be a great challenge for the government to sustain social welfare in its current form without implementing spending cuts. The LDP government's reluctance to implement such measures stem from their electoral concerns. Politically powerful interest groups such as medical associations have opposed welfare spending cuts. So have the LDP *zoku* politicians and the government ministries in charge of social welfare such as the Ministry of Health, Labour and Welfare who would see their budgets and the sources of their regulatory power reduced. In this political situation, welfare spending is more likely to increase, despite the necessity to reduce government debt levels.

Japan will also face challenges in the international economy. Among the most prominent is the continuing rise of China and Japan's engagement in regional economic integration. China' GDP surpassed Japan's in 2010 and its GDP became more than twice Japan's in less than ten years. With greater economic power, China has engaged in economic integration in East Asia with an aim to build a China-centered economic order and exercise greater leadership in the management of the regional economy. For example, the Chinese government established the Asian Infrastructure Investment Bank (AIIB) to finance its infrastructure projects in Asia based on the One Belt One Road Initiative (OBOR). The AIIB is likely to challenge the infrastructure investment from the Asian Development Bank (ADB), which has been dominated by Japan, although there is a scope for cooperation between the two. China's pursuit of the Regional Comprehensive Economic Partnership (RCEP) is also aimed at exercising a greater leadership in trade liberalization and other economic activities in East Asia. Although Japan is also a member of the RCEP, China has more scope to exercise its leadership, as the United States is not a member. Although Japan's pursuit of the Trans-Pacific Partnership (TPP), despite the US withdrawal by the Trump administration, materialised in an agreement on the Comprehensive and Progressive TPP (CPTPP) with other 11 countries in 2018, the issue of how to deal with a rising China and its assertiveness of greater leadership in regional economic integration will remain one of Japan's biggest challenges.

The Japanese economy may not face immediate or rapid decline. However, its challenges need to be overcome. Although politics matters significantly in this respect, there is no guarantee that future Japanese leaders will be able to manage the economy and solve these challenges. Although Japan needs to rid itself of the legacy of the developmental state and reduce the influence of powerful interest groups in order to promote economic efficiency through digitalization, it would also eventually need to establish a more competitive democracy by overcoming the one-party dominance of the LDP and transform itself from a corporate-centered society to a consumer-oriented one.

Notes

1. It was only as late as 1911 that Japan was able to eliminate these unfair commercial treaties by making several amendments.

2. When Hamaguchi's government signed the London Naval Treaty in 1930, it was criticized by the navy, right-wing organizations and the main opposition party as an infringement of the "independence of the supreme command" stipulated in the Meiji Constitution (Berger 1989: 105-07). The Emperor as supreme commander controlled the military and the military was only responsible to the Emperor. In other words, there was no civilian control of the military. The government decision to sign the Treaty against the navy's opposition was criticized for violating the independence of the supreme command.

3. Constitutional amendment needs two-thirds majority in both houses of the Diet (House of the Representatives as the more powerful lower house and the House of Councillors as the less powerful upper house) and a simple majority in a national referendum.

4. Collective wage bargaining by leading companies in each sector conducted each spring – the "Spring Offensive" – was institutionalized in 1955 through the work of labour unions led by Sōhyō (General Council of Trade Unions, the largest national confederation at that time). As a result, the wage increases achieved by leading companies began to spread to smaller companies in each sector.

5. The concept of the "developmental state" is well explained in Chalmers Johnson's book *MITI and the Japanese Miracle*. It will also be examined in Chapter 4 of this book.

6. The idea of introducing a consumption tax was abandoned due to the death of Prime Minister Ōhira.

7. The "six burdens" of the economy were rigid labour markets, highly appreci-

ated yen, high corporate tax, slow progress in forming economic partnerships with foreign countries, strict environmental regulation, and an insufficient amount of electricity provision and its high price (Watanabe 2018a).

8. In March 2011 Japan's northeast coast was pummeled by a massive earthquake and tsunami, triggering a meltdown at the Fukushima Daiichi nuclear power plant.

9. SMEs are classified, in the manufacturing sector, as companies with capital less than ¥300 million or fewer than 300 employees; in the wholesale sector, they are those with capital of less than ¥100 million or fewer than 100 employees; in the service sector, they are those with capital of less than ¥50 million or fewer than 100 employees; and in the case of the retail sector, they are those with capital less than ¥100 million or fewer than 50 employees.

References

Amyx, J. 2004. *Japan's Financial Crisis: Institutional Rigidity and Reluctant Change*. Princeton, NJ: Princeton University Press.

Aoki, K., R. Delbridge & T. Endo 2014. "'Japanese human resource management' in post-bubble Japan". *International Journal of Human Resource Management* 25(18): 2551–72.

Aoki, M. 1999. "Kanryōsei tagenshugi kokka to sangyō soshiki no kyōtsūka" ["Bureaucratic pluralist state and the standardization of the industrial structure"]. In M. Aoki, M. Okuno & T. Okazaki (eds) *Shijō no Yakuwari, Kokka no Yakuwari* [*The Roles of the Government and the Market*]. Tokyo: Tōyō Keizai Shinpōsha.

Aoki, T. 1990. *"Nihon Bunkaron" no Henyō: Sengo Nihon no Bunka to Aidentitī* [*The Transformation of "the Theory of Japanese Culture": The Culture and Identity of Postwar Japan*]. Tokyo: Chūō Kōronsha.

Asahi Shimbun 2015. "Futōkaiko no kinsen kaiketsu o teigen" ["Proposal to introduce fiduciary compensation to deal with unfair dismissal"]. 26 March.

Asahi Shimbun 2016. "Dentsū karōshi mienu kakushin" ["Death due to overwork in Dentsū, unseen essence"]. 27 October.

Asahi Shimbun 2018a. "Gaikokujin rōdō shinzairyū shikaku: Nōgyō, kensetsu nadoni kakudai" ["New visa category for migrant workers: expansion to agriculture, construction, etc."]. 12 October.

Asahi Shimbun 2018b. "Shinzairyū shikaku namanie: Gaikokujin ukeire kakudai raishun tanjun rōdō mo" ["New residential status not discussed enough: expansion of low-skilled foreign workforce next spring"]. 13 October.

Asahi Shimbun 2018c. "Shissō jisshūsei 2870nin kikitori: Hōmushō shūin-i ni teiji" ["Interview with 2870 technical interns who fled from their workplaces:

THE JAPANESE ECONOMY

disclosure to the Legal Affairs Committee in the House of Representatives"].
20 November.

Asahi Shimbun 2018d. "Kaisei nyūkanhō ga kaketsu seiritsu: Gaikokujin rōdōsha no ukeire kakudai". ["The Diet passed the bill on the amendment to the Immigration Control Law: more acceptance of foreign workers"]. 8 December.

Asahi Shimbun 2018e. "Card gizō nihon o hyōteki" ["Targeting Japan with fake cards"]. 25 August.

Asahi Shimbun 2018f. "Netto jōji haishin yōnin NHK no keikaku jōkentsuki de: Yūshikisha kaigi" ["Conditional approval to the NHK plan to simultaneous broadcasting on TV and Internet: Experts meeting"]. 13 July.

Asahi Shimbun 2018g. "Yaku 130man nin ni kashō shikyū: Nenkin kikō kosuto sakugen urame" ["Too little pension payment to about 1.3 million pensioners: cost reduction measure backfired for the Japan Pension Service"]. 27 August.

Asahi Shimbun 2018h. "Rekidai kaichō pasokon tsukaenai: Kakikomi ni Keidanren ga tōwaku" ["Previous chairmen could not use personal computers: Keidanren was perplexed by blogging"]. 26 October.

Asahi Shimbun 2018i. "Sakurada gorinshō wa shisutemu erā: Kaigai media ga hiniku tsugitsugi" [Sakurada Olympic cybersecurity minister suffers from a system error: overseas media ridiculing one after another"]. 16 November.

Asahi Shimbun 2018j. "Judō kinen zero e ippo: Kaiseihō seiritsu, 20nen sekō" ["A step towards zero secondary smoking: an amendment enacted, to be implemented in 2020"]. 19 July.

Asahi Shimbun 2018k. "Hijichikai jūmin wa gomisuteba tsukauna: Toraburu no genba wa" ["Residents who are not members of a neighbourhood association should not use a garbage disposal venue: The situation of the trouble"]. 26 December.

Asahi Shimbun 2018l. "PTA ga kyūshokuhi atsume minō zero demo: Marude Edo jidai" ["PTA collects a school lunch fee despite non-existence of non-payment: as if in the Edo period"]. 31 December.

Asahi Shimbun 2018m. "Shūshoku shishin haishi daigaku mo odoroki" ["The abolishment of the recruitment guideline surprises universities"]. 3 September.

Asahi Shimbun 2019a. "Genpatsu yushutsu koshūshita seiken: Hitachi mo tōketsu, keikaku sōkuzure" ["The Abe administration that insisted the export of nuclear power plants overseas: suspension of the Hitachi project, the total failure of the administration's plans"]. 18 January.

Asahi Shimbun 2019b. "Shushō cashless kessai chotto kinchō shitakedo kantan" ["Prime Minister, a little nervous about using cashless payment although that was easy"]. 2 February.

Asahi Shimbun 2019c. "Nenshū 200man en ga 75 pasento" ["75 percent of non-regular workers' annual income is less than 2 million yen"]. 18 June.

REFERENCES

Asahi Shimbun 2019d. "Inaka de hitohata" ["Success in rural areas"]. 11 February.

Asahi Shimbun 2019e. "Sumaho kessai ni noranu hitobito" ["People who do not use smartphone payment"]. 4 July.

Asahi Shimbun 2019f. "7pay shinki tōroku o teishi" ["7pay suspends new registration for the service"]. 4 July.

Baccaro, L. & C. Howell 2011. "A common neoliberal trajectory: the transformation of industrial relations in advanced capitalism". *Politics & Society* 39(4): 521–63.

Beasley, W. 1989. "The foreign threat and the opening of ports". In M. Jansen (ed.) *The Cambridge History of Japan, Volume 5: Nineteenth Century*. Cambridge: Cambridge University Press.

Becker, G. 1981. "Human capital, effort, and the sexual division of labor". In *A Treatise on the Family*. Cambridge, MA: Harvard University Press.

Beeson, M. 2009. *Institutions of the Asia-Pacific: ASEAN, APEC and Beyond*. Abingdon: Routledge.

Berger, G. 1989. "Politics and mobilization in Japan, 1931-1945". In P. Duus (ed.) *The Cambridge History of Japan, Volume 6: Twentieth Century*. Cambridge: Cambridge University Press.

Boling, P. 1998. "Family policy in Japan". *Journal of Social Policy* 27(2): 173–90.

Boling, P. 2007. "Policies to support working mothers and children in Japan". In F. Rosenbluth (ed.) *The Political Economy of Japan's Low Fertility*. Stanford, CA: Stanford University Press.

Brown, R. Jr. 1999. *The Ministry of Finance: Bureaucratic Practices and the Transformation of the Japanese Economy*. Westport, CT: Quorum Books.

Calder, K. 1993. *Strategic Capitalism: Private Business and Public Purpose in Japanese Industrial Finance*. Princeton, NJ: Princeton University Press.

Cerny, P., G. Menz & S. Soederberg 2005. "Different roads to globalization: neoliberalism, the competition state, and politics in a more open world". In S. Soederberg, G. Menz & P. Cerny (eds) *Internalizing Globalization: The Rise of Neoliberalism and the Decline of National Varieties of Capitalism*. Basingstoke: Palgrave Macmillan.

Chang, H. 1999. "The economic theory of the developmental state". In M. Woo-Cumings (ed.) *The Developmental State*. Ithaca, NY: Cornell University Press.

Cowling, K. & P. Thomlinson 2011. "The Japanese model in retrospective: industrial strategies, corporate Japan and the 'hollowing out' of Japanese industry". *Policy Studies* 32(6): 569–83.

Crawcour, E. 1989a. "Economic change in the nineteenth century". In M. Jansen (ed.) *The Cambridge History of Japan, Volume 5: Nineteenth Century*. Cambridge: Cambridge University Press.

Crawcour, E. 1989b. "Industrialization and technological change: 1885-1920". In P. Duus (ed.) *The Cambridge History of Japan, Volume 6: Twentieth Century.* Cambridge: Cambridge University Press.

Cumings, B. 1999. "Webs with no spiders, spiders with no webs: the genealogy of the developmental state". In M. Woo-Cumings (ed.) *The Developmental State.* Ithaca, NY: Cornell University Press.

Elder, M. 2003. "METI and industrial policy in Japan: change and continuity". In U. Schaede & W. Grimes (eds) *Japan's Managed Globalization: Adapting to the Twenty-first Century.* Armonk, NY: M. E. Sharpe.

Elisonas, J. 1991. "Christianity and the daimyo". In J. Hall (ed.) *The Cambridge History of Japan, Volume 4: Early Modern Japan.* Cambridge: Cambridge University Press.

Emmenegger, P. 2015. "The politics of job security regulations in Western Europe: from drift to layering". *Politics & Society* 43(1): 89–118.

Emmenegger, P., S. Häusermann, B. Palier & M. Seeleib-Kaiser. 2012. "How we grow unequal". In P. Emmenegger, S. Häusermann, B. Palier & M. Seeleib-Kaiser (eds) *The Age of Dualization: The Changing Face of Inequality in Deindustrializing Societies.* Oxford: Oxford University Press.

Friedman, D. 1988. *The Misunderstood Miracle: Industrial Development and Political Change in Japan.* Ithaca, NY: Cornell University Press.

Fukui, H. 1989. "Postwar politics, 1945–1973". In P. Duus (ed.) *The Cambridge History of Japan, Volume 6: Twentieth Century.* Cambridge: Cambridge University Press.

Goishi, N. 2011. *Gendai no Hinkon Wākingu Pua: Koyō to Fukushi no Renkeisaku* [*Contemporary Poverty, Working Poor: The Strategy to Link Employment and Welfare*]. Tokyo: Nihon Keizai Shimbunsha.

Goka, K. 1999. *Koyō no Danryokuka to Rōdōsha Haken, Shokugyō Shōkai Jigyō* [More Flexible Employment and Temporary Agency Work, Job Placement Services]. Tokyo: Ōtsuki Shoten.

Gotō, M. 2011. *Wākingu Pua Genron: Daitenkan to Wakamono* [*Theory of Working Poor: Great Transformation and Young People*]. Tokyo: Kadensha.

Hatch, W. 2010. *Asia's Flying Geese: How Regionalization Shapes Japan.* Ithaca, NY: Cornell University Press.

Hatch, W. & K. Yamamura 1996. *Asia in Japan's Embrace: Building a Regional Production Alliance.* Cambridge: Cambridge University Press.

Hagiwara, K. 2013. "Kodomo teate: Children First no satetsu" ["Child allowance: failure of Children First"]. In Nihon Saiken Initiative (ed.) *Minshutō Seiken Shippai no Kenshō: Nihon Seiji wa Nanio Ikasuka* [*The Failure of the Government of Democratic Party of Japan: What to Learn for Japanese Politics*]. Tokyo: Chūkō Shinsho.

Hall, D. 2004. "Japanese spirit, western economics: the continuing salience of economic nationalism in Japan". In E. Helleiner & A. Pickel (eds) *Economic Nationalism in a Globalizing World*. Ithaca, NY: Cornell University Press.

Hall, J. 1971. *Japan: From Prehistory to Modern Times*. Tokyo: Charles E. Tuttle.

Hall, M. 1998. *Financial Reform in Japan: Causes and Consequences*. Cheltenham: Edward Elgar.

Hall, M. 2007. "Recent banking sector reforms in Japan: An assessment". *Asian Business & Management* 6(1): 57–74.

Hall, P. & D. Soskice 2001. "An introduction to varieties of capitalism". In P. Hall & D. Soskice (eds) *Varieties of Capitalism: The Institutional Foundations of Comparative Advantage*. Oxford: Oxford University Press.

Hall, P. & K. Thelen 2009. "Institutional change in varieties of capitalism". *Socio-Economic Review* 7(1): 7–34.

Hamaaki, J., M. Hori, S. Maeda & K. Murata. 2012. "Changes in the Japanese employment system in the two lost decades". *ILR Review* 65(4): 810–46.

Hane, M. 1992. *Modern Japan: A Historical Survey*. Boulder, CO: Westview Press.

Hasegawa, H. 1993. "Japanese employment practices and industrial relations: the road to union compliance". *Japan Forum* 5(1): 21–35.

Hommerich, C. 2012. "The advent of vulnerability: Japan's free fall through its porous safety net". *Japan Forum* 24(2): 205–32.

Hori, H. 2005. *The Changing Japanese Political System: The Liberal Democratic Party and the Ministry of Finance*. London: Routledge.

House of Councillors, Standing Committee, Special Research Section 1996. "Shōshika taisaku to kongo no kadai" ["The measures to cope with the problem of fewer children and future tasks"]. *Rippō to Chōsa*, March extra issue: 11–16.

Houseman, S. & M. Osawa 2003. "The growth of non-standard employment in Japan and the United States: a comparison of causes and consequences". In S. Houseman & M. Osawa (eds) *Nonstandard Work in Developed Economies: Causes and Consequences*. Kalamazoo, MI: W.E. Upjohn Institute for Employment Research.

Howell, C. & R. Givan 2011. "Rethinking institutions and institutional change in European industrial relations". *British Journal of Industrial Relations* 49(2): 231–55.

Imai, J. 2011. *The Transformation of Japanese Employment Relations: Reform without Labor*. Basingstoke: Palgrave Macmillan.

Industrial Competitiveness Council 2013a. "Kisei kaikaku teian nikansuru genjiten deno kentō jyōkyō" ["The current situation of the discussion on deregulatory proposals"]. 20 September.

Industrial Competitiveness Council 2013b. "'Sekai de toppu reberu no koyō kankyō, hatarakikata' o mezashite" ["In search of a world top-level working environment and situation"]. 17 October.

Industrial Competitiveness Council 2013c. "Dai 4kai Sangyō Kyōsōryoku Kaigi giji yōshi" ["Minutes of the fourth meeting of the Industrial Competitiveness Council"]. 15 March.

Inoguchi, T. & T. Iwai 1987. 'Zokugiin' no Kenkyū: Jimintō Seiken o Gyūjiru Shuyakutachi [Research on 'Zoku Politicians': Main Actors who Control the LDP Government]. Tokyo: Nihon Keizai Shimbunsha.

Ishizawa, Y. 1997. Nihonjinron, Nihonron no Keifu [The Genealogy of the Theory of Japanese, the Theory of Japan]. Tokyo: Maruzen Library.

Ito, M. 2015. Ito Motoshige ga Kataru TPP no Shinjitsu [The Truth of the TPP told by Ito Motoshige]. Tokyo: Nihon Keizai Shimbunsha.

Iwai, H., T. Fukushima, S. Kikuchi & M. Fujie. 2009. Kakusa Shakai no Tōkei Bunseki [Statistical Analysis of the Gap Society]. Sapporo: Hokkaido Daigaku Shuppankai.

Jansen, M. 1989. "The Meiji Restoration". In M. Jansen (ed.) The Cambridge History of Japan, Volume 5: Nineteenth Century. Cambridge: Cambridge University Press.

Japan Times 2017. "69 foreign technical interns died in Japan between 2015 and 2017, ministry data reveals". 7 December.

Japan Times 2018. "Olympic embarrassment: Japan falls way short in banning public smoking ahead of 2020 Games". 6 February.

Johnson, C. 1982. MITI and the Japanese Miracle: The Growth of Industrial Policy, 1925–1975. Stanford, CA: Stanford University Press.

Johnson, C. 1999. "The developmental state: odyssey of a concept". In M. Woo-Cumings (ed.) The Developmental State. Ithaca, NY: Cornell University Press.

Kageyama, K. 1994. "Nihongata keiei raisanron no meian" ["The bright and dark sides of the worship theory of Japanese management"]. In K. Uchihashi, H. Okumura & M. Sataka (eds) Nihon Kaisha Genron 1: Kiki nonakano Nihon Kigyō [Theory of Japanese companies 1: Japanese Companies in the Crisis]. Tokyo: Iwanami Shoten.

Kalinowski, T. 2015. "Crisis management and the diversity of capitalism: fiscal stimulus packages and the East Asian (neo-)developmental state". Economy and Society 44(2): 244–70.

Kawanishi, Y. 2008. "On karo-jisatsu (suicide by overwork): why do Japanese workers work themselves to death?". International Journal of Mental Health 37(1): 61–74.

Kawahito, H. 2014. Karō Jisatsu [Death Due to Overwork]. Tokyo: Iwanami Shinsho.

Kitaoka, S. 1995. *Jimintō: Seikentō no 38nen* [*The Liberal Democratic Party: 38 Years of the Governing Party*]. Tokyo: Yomiuri Shimbunsha.

Kitschelt, H. *et al.* 1999. "Convergence and divergence in advanced capitalist democracies". In H. Kitschelt (eds) *Continuity and Change in Contemporary Capitalism*. Cambridge: Cambridge University Press.

Kohno. M. 2003. "A changing Ministry of International Trade and Industry". In J. Amyx & J. Drysdale (eds) *Japanese Governance: Beyond Japan Inc.* London: Routledge Curzon.

Korpi, W. 1983. *The Democratic Class Struggle*. London: Routledge & Kegan Paul.

Korpi, W. 2006. "Power resources and employer-centered approaches in explanations of welfare states and varieties of capitalism: protagonists, consenters, and antagonists". *World Politics* 58(2): 167–206.

Kōsai, Y. 1989. "The postwar Japanese economy, 1945–1973". In P. Duus (ed.) *The Cambridge History of Japan, Volume 6: Twentieth Century*. Cambridge: Cambridge University Press.

Kōseishō 1999a. *Shōshika Taisaku notameno Rinji Tokubetsu Kōfukin nikansuru Kōfu Yōkō* [Synopsis of the provision of temporary special subsidies as a measure to cope with the problem of fewer children].

Kōseishō 1999b. *Shōshika Taisaku notameno Rinji Tokubetsu Kōfukin nikansuru Jisshi Yōkō* [Synopsis of the implementation of temporary special subsidies as a measure to cope with the problem of fewer children].

Kremers, D. 2014. "Transnational migrant advocacy from Japan: tipping the scales in the policy-making process". *Pacific Affairs* 87(4): 715–41.

Kujiraoka, H. 2016. *Dokyumento TPP Kōshō: Ajia Keizai Haken no Yukue* [*Documentary on the TPP Negotiation: The Future Hegemony in the Asia-Pacific Economy*]. Tokyo: Tōyō Keizai Shinpōsha.

Kumazawa, 2000. *Josei Rōdō to Kigyō Shakai* [*Female Labour and Corporate Society*]. Tokyo: Iwanami Shoten.

Kume, I. 1998. *Disparaged Success: Labor Politics in Postwar Japan*. Ithaca, NY: Cornell University Press.

Kume, I. 2000. "Institutionalizing post-war Japanese political economy: industrial policy revisited". In K. Brodsgaard & S. Young (eds) *State Capacity in East Asia: Japan, Taiwan, China and Vietnam*. Oxford: Oxford University Press.

Kume, I. 2005. *Rōdō Seiji: Sengo Seiji no nakano Rōdō Kumiai* [*Labour Politics: Labour Unions in Postwar Politics*]. Tokyo: Chūkō Shinsho.

Lam, A. 1992. *Women and Japanese Management: Discrimination and Reform*. London: Routledge.

Lam, A. 1993. "Equal employment opportunities for Japanese women: changing company practice". In J. Hunter (ed.) *Japanese Women Working*. London: Routledge.

Levi-Faur, D. 1997. "Friedrich List and the political economy of the nation-state". *Review of International Political Economy* 4(1): 154–78.

Maclachlan, P. 2011. "Ideas, interests and institutions: Japanese postal privatization in comparative perspective". In L. Schoppa (ed.) *The Evolution of Japan's Party System: Politics and Policy in an Era of Institutional Change*. Toronto: University of Toronto Press.

Mason, M. 1999. "Japan's low levels of inward direct investment". In P. Drysdale & L. Gower (eds) *The Japanese Economy, Part 2: Volume VII: Technologies, Foreign Investment and Competition Policies*. London: Routledge.

Michinaka, T. 2009. *Seikatsu Hogo to Nihongata Wākingu Pua: Hinkon no Koteika to Sedaikan Keishō* [*Social Assistance and Japanese-Style Working Poor: The Institutionalization of Poverty and Generational Transfer*]. Kyoto: Minerva Shobō.

Milhaupt, C. 1999. "Japan's experience with deposit insurance and falling banks: implications for financial regulatory design?". IMES Discussion Paper No. 99-E-8, Institute for Monetary and Economic Studies. Tokyo: Bank of Japan.

Miura, M. 2012. *Welfare through Work: Conservative Ideas, Partisan Dynamics, and Social Protection in Japan*. Ithaca, NY: Cornell University Press.

Miwa, Y. 1995. "Policies for small business in Japan". In H. Kim (ed.) *The Japanese Civil Service and Economic Development: Catalyst of Change*. Oxford: Oxford University Press.

Moriguchi, C. 2014. "Japanese-style human resource management and its historical origins". *Japan Labor Review* 11(3): 58–77.

Moriguchi, C. & H. Ono 2006. "Japanese lifetime employment: a century's perspective". In M. Blomstrom & S. La Coix (eds) *Institutional Change in Japan*. London: Routledge.

Morioka, K. 2005. *Hatarakisugino Jidai* [*The Era of Overwork*]. Tokyo: Iwanami Shinsho.

Morioka, K. 2009. *Hinkonka suru Howaito Karā* [*White-Collar Workers who are Becoming Impoverished*]. Tokyo: Chikuma Shinsho.

Morioka, K. 2015. *Koyō Mibun Shakai* [*Employment Status Society*]. Tokyo: Iwanami Shinsho.

Mouer. R. & H. Kawanishi 2005. *A Sociology of Work in Japan*. Cambridge: Cambridge University Press.

Nagano, K. 1994. "Nihonteki kōporēto gabanansu no michi: Nichibei hikaku no shiten kara" ["Japanese-style corporate governance: from a comparative perspective of the US and Japan"]. In K. Uchihashi, H. Okumura & M. Sataka (eds) *Nihon Kaisha Genron 1: Kiki nonakano Nihon Kigyō* [*Theory of Japanese Companies 1: Japanese Companies in the Crisis*]. Tokyo: Iwanami Shoten.

Nakagawa, J. 2006. "Taigai keizai seisaku: Nichibei kōzō kyōgi kara higashi ajia kyōdōtai e" ["Foreign economic policy: From the US-Japan Structural Initiative to East Asian Community"]. In Tokyo Daigaku Shakai Kagaku Kenkyūjo (ed.) *Ushinawareta 10nen o Koete II: Koizumi Kaikaku eno Jidai* [*Beyond a Lost Decade: The Era Towards Koizumi Reform*]. Tokyo: Tokyo Daigaku Shuppankai.

Nakamura, K. & M. Miura 2005. "Chihō Rengō no chōsen" [Challenges for Regional Rengō]. In K. Nakamura & Rengō Sōgō Kaihatsu Kenkyūjo (eds) *Suitai ka Saisei ka: Rōdō Kumiai Kasseika eno Michi* [*Decline or Revival: Towards the Revitalization of Labour Unions*]. Tokyo: Keisō Shobō.

Nakamura, T. 1989. "Depression, recovery, and war, 1920-1945". In P. Duus (ed.) *The Cambridge History of Japan, Volume 6: Twentieth Century*. Cambridge: Cambridge University Press.

Naughton, B. 1999. "China: Domestic restricting and a new role in Asia". In T. Pempel (ed.) *The Politics of the Asian Economic Crisis*. Ithaca, NY: Cornell University Press.

Nemoto, K. 2013. "Long working hours and the corporate gender divide in Japan". *Gender, Work & Organization* 20(5): 512–27.

Nihon Keizai Shimbun 2013a. "Renesas 'kansei saisei' hayakumo teitai" ["'Bureaucratic revitalization' of Renesas has stagnated too soon"]. 16 April.

Nihon Keizai Shimbun 2013b. "Seichō senryaku kantei ga shudō: Kisei kanwa ya TPP taisaku" ["The Cabinet leads the growth strategy: the measures for deregulation and the TPP"]. 1 March.

Nihon Keizai Shimbun 2013c. "Sekai saisentan IT kokka e: Seifu senryaku nitaisuru gyōkai no honne" ["Towards the world No.1 IT nation: the industry's real opinion on the government strategy"]. 27 June.

Nihon Keizai Shimbun 2015. "Credit card subete IC gata ni: Visa nado 20nen madeni" ["IC chips in all credit cards: Visa and other credit card companies aim to achieve it by 2020"]. 26 July.

Nihon Keizai Shimbun 2016. "Sharp saiken Hon Hai jikuni: Oitsumerareta hinomaru" ["The restructuring of Sharp will be based on the acquisition by Hon Hai: the Japanese government in a pinch"]. 4 February.

Nihon Keizai Shimbun 2017. "Toshiba nichibeikan to handōtai baikyaku keiyaku: Nihonzei ga kahan shusshi" ["Toshiba concludes a sales agreement on Toshiba Memory with the Japan, US and South Korean investors"]. 28 September.

Nihon Keizai Shimbun 2018a. "Uber nihon de taxi haisha ni senryaku tenkai" ["Uber has changed its business strategy in Japan and engage in taxi dispatch service"]. 19 February.

Nihon Keizai Shimbun 2018b. "Son-shi ga hokoru ride-share rengō nihon no kabe" ["Japanese wall against the ride-sharing business alliance Mr Son is proud of"]. 3 October.

Nihon Keizai Shimbun 2018c. "Tōi cashless senshinkoku" ["Far behind cashless developed countries"]. 24 December.

Nihon Keizai Shimbun 2018d. "Card tesūryō jōgen 3pacentodai: Shōhi zōzeiji ni seifu yōsei" ["The highest credit card fee around 3 per cent: government request at the time of consumption tax hike"]. 20 October.

Nihon Keizai Shimbun 2018e. "Hōnichi visa netto uketsuke: Mazu chūgoku dantaikyaku ni" ["Internet application for a Japanese tourist visa: for Chinese tourist groups to begin with"]. 2 September.

Nihon Keizai Shimbun 2019a. "Shōwa na shokuba to teiseichō: Dejitaruka ga nihon no jakuten" ["Workplace like in a Shōwa era and low economic growth: digitalization as a Japan's weak point"]. 8 July.

Nihon Keizai Shimbun 2019b. "Nihon no genpatsu fukurokōji ni: Kaigai anken zero" ["The cul-de-sac of Japan's nuclear power industry: the number of overseas projects has become zero"]. 12 January.

Nihon Keizai Shimbun 2019c. "RCEP nennai daketsu dannen: Indo ga teikō ridatsu mo shisa" ["Agreement on the RCEP abandoned in 2019: India refused and even suggested its withdrawal"]. 4 November.

Nishikawa, K. 2017. *TPP no Shinjitsu: Sōdai na Kyōtei o Matomeageta Otokotachi* [*The Truth of the TPP: The Men Who Created the Grandiose Agreement*]. Tokyo: Kaitakusha.

Nishinarita, Y. 1998. "Japanese-style industrial relations in a historical perspective". In H. Hasegawa & G. Hook (eds) *Japanese Business Management: Restructuring for Low Growth and Globalization*. London: Routledge.

Nishitani, S. 2014. "Zenmentekina kiseikanwa kōsei to rōdōhō no kiki" ["Wholesale deregulatory attack and the crisis of the labour law"]. In S. Nishitani et al. (eds) *Nihon no Koyō ga Abunai: Abe Seiken "Rōdō Kisei Kanwa" Hihan* [*Japanese Employment in Danger: Critique of the Abe Administration's Labour Deregulation*]. Tokyo: Junpōsha.

Noguchi, Y. 1998. "The 1940 system: Japan under the wartime economy". *American Economic Review* 88(2): 404-07.

Nomura, M. 1994. "Shūshin koyōsei giron no kansei" ["The trap in the debate on lifetime employment"]. In K. Uchihashi, H. Okumura & M. Sataka (eds) *Nihon Kaisha Genron 1: Kiki nonakano Nihon Kigyō* [*Theory of Japanese Companies 1: Japanese Companies in the Crisis*]. Tokyo: Iwanami Shoten.

North, S. & R. Morioka 2016. "Hope found in lives lost: Karoshi and the pursuit of worker rights in Japan". *Contemporary Japan* 28(1): 59-80.

Norville, E. 1998. "The 'illiberal' roots of Japanese financial regulatory reform". In L. Carlile & M. Tilton (eds) *Is Japan Really Changing Its Ways? Regulatory Reform and the Japanese Economy*. Washington, DC: Brookings Institution Press.

Ogura, K. 2013. *'Seishain' no Kenkyū* [Research on Regular Workers]. Tokyo: Nihon Keizai Shimbunsha.

Okazaki, T. 1999. "Sengo nihon no sangyō seisaku to seifu soshiki" ["The industrial policy and the government organization in postwar Japan"]. In M. Aoki, M. Okuno & T. Okazaki (eds) *Shijō no Yakuwari, Kokka no Yakuwari [The Roles of the Government and the Market]*. Tokyo: Tōyō Keizai Shinpōsha.

Okimoto, D. 1989. *Between MITI and the Market: Japanese Industrial Policy for High Technology*. Stanford, CA: Stanford University Press.

Okumura, H. 1994. "Nihongata kigyō shisutemu" ["Japanese-style corporate system"]. In K. Uchihashi, H. Okumura & M. Sataka (eds) *Nihon Kaisha Genron 2: Nihongata Keiei to Kokusai Shakai [Theory of Japanese Companies 2: Japanese-Style Management and the International Society]*. Tokyo: Iwanami Shoten.

Onuki, H. 2009. "Care, social (re)production and global labour migration: Japan's 'special gift' toward 'innately gifted' Filipino workers". *New Political Economy* 14(4): 489–516.

Osawa, M. 1993. *Kigyō Chūshin Shakai o Koete: Gendai Nihon o Jendā de Yomu [Beyond Corporate-Centered Society: Analyzing Contemporary Japan Through Gender]*. Tokyo: Jiji Tsūshinsha.

Osawa, M. 1996. "Shakai seisaku no jendā baiasu: Nikkan hikaku no kokoromi" ["Gender bias in social policy: Comparison of Japan and Korea"]. In H. Hara, M. Maeda & M Osawa (eds) *Ajia Taiheiyō Chiiki no Josei Seisaku to Joseigaku [Women Policies and Women Studies in Asia-Pacific]*. Tokyo: Shinyōsha.

Osawa, M. 1999. "Japanese-style employment practices and male-female wage differentials". In K. Sato (ed.) *The Transformation of the Japanese Economy*. Armonk, NY: M. E. Sharpe.

Osawa, M. 2003. "Kakusa/byōdōron to shakai seisaku no kaikaku: Jendā no shiten kara" [The discussion on inequality/equality and the reform of social policy: from a gender perspective"]. In Y. Higuchi & Zaimushō Zaimu Sōgō Seisaku Kenkyūjo (eds) *Nihon no Shotoku Kakusa to Shakai Kaisō [The Income Gap and Social Stratification in Japan]*. Tokyo: Nihon yōronsha.

Osawa, M. 2009. "Nihon no pāto rōdōsha to josei rōdōsha no hiseishainka" ["Part-time workers in Japan and women workers becoming non-regular workers"]. In E. Takeishi (ed.) *Josei no Hatarakikata [How Women Work]*. Kyoto: Minerva Shobō.

Osawa, M. 2010. *Nihongata Wākingu Pua no Honshitsu: Tayōsei o Tsutsumikomi*

Ikasu Shakai e [*The Essence of the Japanese-Style Working Poor: Towards a Society Accepting Diversity*]. Tokyo: Iwanami Shoten.

Osawa, M., M. Kim & J. Kingston 2013. "Precarious work in Japan". *American Behavioral Scientist* 57(3): 309–34.

Palier, B. & K. Thelen 2010. "Institutionalizing dualism: complementarities and change in France and Germany". *Politics & Society* 38(1): 119–48.

Pempel, T. 1999a. "The developmental regime in a changing world economy". In M. Woo-Cumings (ed.) *The Developmental State*. Ithaca, NY: Cornell University Press.

Pempel, T. 1999b. "Conclusion". In T. Pempel (ed.) *The Politics of the Asian Economic Crisis*. Ithaca, NY: Cornell University Press.

Pempel, T. 2012. "Between pork and productivity: upending the Japanese model of capitalism". In M. Ido (ed.) *Varieties of Capitalism, Types of Democracy and Globalization*. Abingdon: Routledge.

Roberts, G. 2018. "An immigration policy in *any* other name: semantics of immigration to Japan". *Social Science Japan Journal* 21(1): 89–102.

Rosenbluth, F. 2007. "The political economy of low fertility". In F. Rosenbluth (ed.) *The Political Economy of Japan's Low Fertility*. Stanford, CA: Stanford University Press.

Rueda, D. 2007. *Social Democracy Inside Out: Partisanship and Labor Market Policy in Advanced Industrialized Democracies*. Oxford: Oxford University Press.

Samuels, R. 1987. *The Business of the Japanese State: Energy Markets in Comparative and Historical Perspective*. Ithaca, NY: Cornell University Press.

Streeck, W. 2009. *Re-Forming Capitalism: Institutional Change in the German Political Economy*. Oxford: Oxford University Press.

Stubbs, R. 2009. "Whatever happened to the East Asian developmental state? The unfolding debate". *Pacific Review* 22(1): 1–22.

Sugimoto, Y. 2003. *An Introduction to Japanese Society*. Cambridge: Cambridge University Press.

Suzuki, A. 2006. "Sanbetsu soshiki no soshiki kakudai senryaku: Sono seidoteki bunmyaku to baikai yōin" ["Organizing strategies of industrial federations: institutional context and intervening factors"]. In A. Suzuki & S. Hayakawa (eds) *Rōdō Kumiai no Soshiki Kakudai Senryaku* [*Organizing Strategies of Labour Unions*]. Tokyo: Ochanomizu Shobō.

Suzuki, A. 2012. "The limits and possibilities of social movement unionism in Japan in the context of industrial relations institutions". In A. Suzuki (ed.) *Cross-National Comparisons of Social Movement Unionism: Diversities of Labour Movement Revitalization in Japan, Korea and the United States*. Oxford: Peter Lang.

Tachibanaki, T. 2004. *Datsu Frītā Shakai* [*Escape from a Freeter Society*]. Tokyo: Tōyō Keizai Shinpōsha.

Taira, K. 1989. "Economic development, labor markets, and industrial relations in Japan, 1905–1955". In P. Duus (ed.) *The Cambridge History of Japan, Volume 6: Twentieth Century*. Cambridge: Cambridge University Press.

Takahashi, Y. 2006. "Unpaid overtime for white-collar workers". *Japan Labor Review* 3(3): 41–54.

Thelen, K. 2009. "Institutional change in advanced political economies". *British Journal of Industrial Relations* 47(3): 471–98.

Thelen, K. 2014. *Varieties of Liberalization and the New Politics of Social Solidarity*. Cambridge: Cambridge University Press.

Thelen, K. & I. Kume 1999. "The effects of globalization on labor revisited: lessons from Germany and Japan". *Politics & Society* 27(4): 477–505.

Thelen, K. & I. Kume 2006. "Coordination as a political problem in coordinated market economies". *Governance* 19(1): 11–42.

Tilton, M. & H. Choi 2007. "Legacies of the developmental state for Japan's information and communications industries". In C. Storz & A. Moerke (eds) *Competitiveness of New Industries: Institutional Framework and Learning in Information Technology in Japan, the US and Germany*. London: Routledge.

Tochio, I. 2000. "Kosodate shien sesaku: 90 nenndai niokeru seido kaikaku to sono hyōka" ["Supporting measures for child-rearing: institutional reform in the 1990s and its evaluation"]. *Sekai no Jidō to Bosei* 48: 14–17.

Toya, T. 2006. *The Political Economy of the Japanese Financial Big Bang: Institutional Change in Finance and Pubic Policymaking*. Oxford: Oxford University Press.

Urano, E. & P. Stewart 2007. "Including the excluded workers? The challenges of Japan's Kanagawa City Union". *WorkingUSA: Journal of Labor and Society* 10: 103–23.

Uriu, R. 1996. *Troubled Industries: Confronting Economic Change in Japan*. Ithaca, NY: Cornell University Press.

Vogel, E. 1979. *Japan as Number One: Lessons for America*. Cambridge, MA: Harvard University Press.

Wada, J. 2007. "The political economy of daycare centers in Japan". In F. Rosenbluth (ed.) *The Political Economy of Japan's Low Fertility*. Stanford, CA: Stanford University Press.

Waswo, A. 1989. "The transformation of rural society, 1900–1950". In P. Duus (ed.) *The Cambridge History of Japan, Volume 6: Twentieth Century*. Cambridge: Cambridge University Press.

Watanabe, H. 2012. "Why and how did Japan finally change its ways? The politics of Japanese labour-market deregulation since the 1990s". *Japan Forum* 24(1): 23–50.

Watanabe, H. 2014. *Labour Market Deregulation in Japan and Italy: Worker Protection Under Neoliberal Globalisation*. London: Routledge.

Watanabe, H. 2015a. "Neoliberal reform for greater competitiveness: labour market deregulation in Japan and Italy". *Industrial Relations Journal* 46(1): 54–76.

Watanabe, H. 2015b. "The struggle for revitalisation by Japanese labour unions: worker organising after labour-market deregulation". *Journal of Contemporary Asia* 45(3): 510–30.

Watanabe, H. 2015c. "Institutional change under neoliberal pressure: Japanese regulatory reforms in labor and financial markets after the collapse of the bubble economy". *Asian Politics & Policy* 7(3): 413–32.

Watanabe, H. 2018a. "Labour market dualism and diversification in Japan". *British Journal of Industrial Relations* 56(3): 579–602.

Watanabe, H. 2018b. "Political agency and social movements of Japanese individually-affiliated unions". *Economic and Industrial Democracy* 1–21, doi. org/10.1177/0143831X18789794 (online first).

Weathers, C. & S. North 2009. "Overtime activists take on corporate titans: Toyota, McDonald's and Japan's work hour controversy". *Pacific Affairs* 82(4): 615–36.

Westney, D. 1999. "The Japanese business system: key features and prospects for change". In P. Drysdale & L. Gower (eds) *The Japanese Economy, Part 1: Volume IV: The Nature of the Japanese Firm*. London: Routledge.

Woo-Cumings, M. 1999. "Introduction: Chalmers Johnson and the politics of nationalism and development". In M. Woo-Cumings (ed.) *The Developmental State*. Ithaca, NY: Cornell University Press.

Woodall, B. 1996. *Japan under Construction: Corruption, Politics, and Public Works*. Berkeley, CA: University of California Press.

Yamada, M. 2007. *Shōshi Shakai Nihon: Mōhitotsuno Kakusano Yukue* [*Few Children Society Japan: Another Result of Inequality*]. Tokyo: Iwanami Shinsho.

Yamada, M. 2009. *Wākingu Pua Jidai: Sokonuke Sēfutī Net o Saikōtchiku seyo* [*Working Poor Era: Rebuild the Porous Safety Net*]. Tokyo: Bungei Shunjū.

Index